»Lasst uns mit den Konventionen brechen, nehmen wir uns die Freiheit zum eigenen, individuellen Stil. Und schaffen wir unsere eigenen Regeln«

Inspired by Karl Lagerfeld

“Let’s break with conventions, let’s take the liberty of having our own individual style. And let’s make own rules.”

TABLE COUTURE THE MIX

BY PETRA DIENERS

AND MATCH
TABLE
STYLE
BOOK

INCLUDING STORIES ABOUT TABLE COUTURE FOR HOSTS AND GUESTS

BY INGO KABUTZ

Contents

P
E
A
C
E

Editorial

Dieses Buch widmen wir allen, die sich ebenso für schön gedeckte Tische und für eine herzliche und gepflegte Gastlichkeit begeistern. TABLE COUTURE wendet sich auch an die neue Generation von kreativen Freigeistern, die – ähnlich wie in der Mode – ihre Freiheitsliebe und ihre Kreativität auch beim Table Setting ausleben möchten. Unser Vorschlag schon jetzt: Nutze das Buch als Style Guide für deine ganz individuellen Table Stylings und werde auch du Table Couturier.

Lass uns gemeinsam die kreative Poesie des Mix and Match entdecken. Sie ist der Schlüssel für eine neue Table-Culture-Ästhetik, mit der du sofort beginnen und deinen ganz persönlichen Stil entwickeln kannst. Lasst uns in diesem Buch gemeinsam den Tisch decken – je nach Anlass und Jahreszeit. Und von Zeit zu Zeit überlegen wir uns passende Outfits, in denen wir uns wirklich wohlfühlen, wenn die Familie, wenn Freunde oder Gäste zusammenkommen. Denn für uns ist das Allerwichtigste: Sich entspannt und mit Muße den Gästen widmen zu können.

Es ist uns ein Vergnügen, dir einige ebenso vergnügliche wie lehrreiche Facetten der Tafelkultur näherzubringen.

We dedicate this book to all those who are as enthusiastic about beautifully laid tables and sophisticated, welcoming hospitality as we are. TABLE COUTURE also addresses the new generation of creative free spirits who - similar to the current fashion trends - want to live out their love of freedom and their creativity through table settings as we are. Our suggestion: Use the book as a style guide for your own individual table stylings and become a table couturier.

Let‘s discover the creative poetry of mixing and matching together. It's the key to a new table culture aesthetic that you can start using immediately in order to develop your own unique, personal style. In this book, let's set the table together - depending on the occasion and the season. And togehter we will think about suitable outfits that make us feel truly comfortable when our family, friends, or guests get together. Because for us, the most important thing is to be able to relax and enjoy our guests.

It is our pleasure to introduce you to some aspects of table culture that are as enjoyable as they are educational.

Yours sincerely

Petra Dieners

Redefining the ultimate art of table setting

Table Couture

A new generation of creative hosts is redifining the art of table setting. The resulting TABLE COUTURE is rapidly becoming the gold standard for creative tablescapes.

This new generation of hosts shares the same values and passion as the generations before them: they value their guests and and enhance special occasions with elegant, stylish table settings. Today, however, hosts are not only concerned with presenting iconic products from outstanding manufacturers in a stylish way for various occasions.

Just as in fashion, this new generation also wants to live out their individual creativity and freedom through table settings. Using a liberal mix-and-match approach, they combine their tried-and-true favorites, heirlooms, and/or individual pieces with newly acquired "table icons." This is how TABLE COUTURE tablescapes are created: a unique new poetry, power, and charisma that emerges from table couturiers mixing and matching seemingly contradictory designs and formal languages and brought to life by the new freedom to be creative and to develop one's own personal style.

Eine neue Generation von kreativen Gastgeberinnen und Gastgebern verändert die Definition der Tischkultur. Die daraus entstehende TABLE COUTURE entwickelt sich rasant zur Königsdisziplin für den gedeckten Tisch.

Mit den Generationen vor ihnen teilen die neuen GastgeberInnen die Werte und die Leidenschaft, mit stilvoll-edel gedeckten Tafeln ihre Gäste wertzuschätzen und den Anlass zu adeln. Heute geht es den GastgeberInnen aber nicht nur darum, die ikonischen Produkte herausragenderw Manufakturen für die unterschiedlichen Anlässe stilvoll zu präsentieren.

Diese neue Generation will – ebenso wie in der Mode – auch beim Table Setting ihre individuelle Kreativität und Freiheit ausleben. Unter Anwendung des freiheitlich-liberalen Mix and Match kombinieren sie ihre langjährigen Lieblings-Services, Erb- oder/und Einzelstücke mit neu erworbenen „Table Icons". So entstehen Inszenierungen der TABLE COUTURE: eine einzigartige neue Poesie, Kraft und Ausstrahlung, die durch das Mixen und Matchen scheinbar gegensätzlicher Designs und Formsprachen der Table Couturiers entsteht. Zum Leben erweckt durch die neue Freiheit zur eigenen Kreativität und zur ganz persönlichen Stilentwicklung.

Petra Dieners

Petra Dieners steht für die Werte und die Kreativität der TABLE COUTURE.

Die international erfolgreiche Luxury-Lifestyle Influencerin inszeniert für dieses Buch klassische und aktuelle Produkt-Ikonen internationaler Porzellan-Manufakturen. Mit ihren kreativen Styling-Ideen inspiriert sie auch die neue Gastgebergeneration.

Dieses innovative Table Stylebook weckt die neue Lust auf den stilvoll gedeckten Tisch für die bedeutsamen Momente im Leben.

Petra Dieners represents the values and creativity of TABLE COUTURE.

For this book the successful luxury lifestyle influencer has combined classic and current product icons from international luxury manufacturers. With her creative styling ideas, she has set out to inspires the new generation of hosts.

This innovative guide aims to inspire and encourage hosts to set uniquely stylish tables for life's important moments.

Sincerely yours

Ingo Kabutz

Roots

Schon als Kind habe ich bei meiner Tante andächtig vor der Porzellanvitrine gestanden und das „weiße Gold" bewundert. Einen Unterschied gibt es zu früher: Im Gegensatz zu meiner Tante benutze ich das gute Geschirr täglich. Und zwar in allen Facetten.

Ich liebe Geschirr und schön gedeckte Tische. Dabei bin ich nicht festgelegt auf modern oder nostalgisch, reduziert oder opulent. Je nach Lust, Laune und Stimmung dekoriere ich die Tische so, wie mir gerade der Sinn steht. Altes Porzellan mag ich genauso gerne wie neues.

Wie in der Mode macht es mir unglaublichen Spaß, Porzellane zu kombinieren. Zum Beispiel einen alten Speiseteller mit einem modernen Vorspeisenteller zu mischen und immer wieder neue Tischdekorationen zu kreieren.

Even as a child, I used to stand reverently in front of my aunt's porcelain display case and admire the "white gold" within. But today, there's one big difference: Unlike my aunt, I use the good china every day in all sorts of ways.

I love dishes and beautifully set tables. But I'm not limited to modern or nostalgic, minimalist or opulent. Depending on my mood, I decorate my table based on how I'm feeling in that moment. I like old porcelain just as much as new.

Just like with fashion, I have so much fun combining porcelains. For example, I love pairing an old dinner plate with a modern appetizer plate in order to constantly create new and changing tablescapes.

Let's

create

Ich nehme dich mit in mein Zuhause. Mit meinen Styling-Ideen führe ich dich durch die Jahreszeiten. Wir überlegen uns, welche Table Stylings am besten zu welchen Festen und besonderen Anlässen passen. Ich freue mich darauf, gemeinsam mit dir kreativ zu werden.

Du wirst meine Leidenschaft bald teilen und dein altes, fast vergessenes Service aus dem Schrank holen und neu in Szene setzen. Es ist an der Zeit, diese Tradition für sich neu zu entdecken, diese wunderbare Handarbeit wieder zu schätzen und ihr im Sinne der Nachhaltigkeit ein „neues Leben" zu ermöglichen.

Ich danke meinen Liebsten, die mich bei meinen kreativen Ideen immer unterstützen und meine Sammelleidenschaft mal mehr, mal weniger dulden.

And now I'm inviting you into my home. With my styling ideas, I will guide you through the seasons. We will consider which table stylings are best suited to which celebrations and special occasions. I look forward to being creative with you.

Soon you too will share my passion for table settings and take your old, nearly forgotten dishes out of the cupboard so they can shine. Now, it's time to rediscover this tradition for yourself, to appreciate this wonderful handicraft again, and to give your old dishes a "new life" that is both sustainable and stylish!

I would like to thank my loved ones, who always support my creative ideas and more or less tolerate my passion for collecting.

FALL SETTINGS

Rendezvous with a lady

Schon vor Jahren habe ich mir das Fornasetti Porzellan gekauft. Obwohl die Sammelteller eigentlich Wandteller sind, benutze ich sie als Vorspeisen- oder Dessertteller. Durch die unterschiedlichen Motive, aber die gleiche Farbgestaltung wirkt der Tisch sehr lebendig und interessant.

Hier habe ich die Teller in Kombination mit meinem allerersten Geschirr von Limoges, ein schlichtes Service mit Goldrand, und Platztellern von Reichenbach kombiniert.

Die Teller habe ich auf Tischläufern im Fischgratmuster von Gabriele Hofer platziert und die Farben Orange und Pink mit aufgenommen. Die Gläser stehen abwechselnd in Pink und Orange auf dem Tisch. Das Farbspiel ist ergänzt mit orangefarbenen Servietten und Windlichtern in Orange.

Auch Gläser und Servietten in Türkis würden wunderbar zu dieser Porzellankombination passen.

Years ago, I purchased a set of Fornasetti porcelain. Although the collectible plates are actually wall plates, I use them as appetizer or dessert plates. Combining different motifs within the same color scheme gives the table a lively, interesting look.

Here, I have combined the plates from combination with my very first Limoges dinnerware, a plain service with a gold rim, and charger plates from Reichenbach.

I arranged the plates on table runners in with a herringbone pattern by Gabriele Hofer and included the colors orange and pink. The glasses are arranged on the table alternately in pink and orange. The play of colors is complemented by orange napkins and orange candleholders.

Turquoise glassware and napkins would also go wonderfully with this china combination.

tip charger plates

1 Platzteller sollten auf keiner schön gedeckten Tafel fehlen. Die Tischdekoration sieht vollständiger, harmonischer und edler aus.

Charger plates are an absolute must for any beautifully set table. They make the table look complete, harmonious, and elegant.

2 Die Platzteller von Reichenbach sind eigentlich Kuchenplatten, aber sie eignen sich wunderbar als Platzteller und passen zu jedem anderen Service.

The Reichenbach charger plates seen here are actually cake plates, but they are wonderful as charger plates and go well with any other service.

This fall will definitely be different

tip Wine

Man muss kein Sommelier sein, um den passenden Wein zu finden. Wir lieben zu italienischen Vorspeisen zum Beispiel einen Roero Arneis aus dem Piemont – speziell von dem Erzeuger Bruno Giacosa . Bei Rotweinen favorisieren wir u.a. die Spanier aus dem Priorat.

You don't have to be a sommelier to find the right wine. We love for example Roero Arneis from Piemont – espacially from the winemaker Bruno Giacosa – with Italian starters. With red wines, we favour the Spanish from the Priorat.

MODERN & COZY

Japan Print – ein modernes Porzellan mit traditionellen Elementen. Pink und viel Gold. Die Teller stammen aus einer Kollektion von Paola Navone von Reichenbach.

Die unterschiedlichen Teller ergeben zusammen ein perfektes Bild. Dazu kombiniere ich mein Goldbesteck und klassische Weingläser.

Als Akzent und Kontrast stelle ich schwarze Wassergläser von Rotter Glas dazu. Das Design des Glases mit dem Drachenmotiv passt zu der Wahl des Porzellans.

Die taupefarbenen Tischläufer (Gabriele Hofer) auf der weißen Tischdecke lassen die gesamte Tischdekoration und das Gold richtig strahlen.

Japan Print - a modern porcelain design with traditional elements. Pink and lots of gold. The plates are from a collection by Paola Navone for Reichenbach.

When combined, the different plates create a perfect picture. In addition, I add my gold cutlery and classic wine glasses.

As an accent and contrast, I have chosen to use black water glasses from Rotter Glas. The black glasses feature a dragon motif that pairs perfectly with the porcelain.

The taupe table runners (Gabriele Hofer) on the white tablecloth let the entire table decoration and the gold really shine.

Das Pink der Servietten, Vasen und Kerzenständer spiegelt sich im großen Speiseteller wider und harmoniert mit dem Gold.

Die Seidenarmbänder aus Hermès Tüchern habe ich „zweckentfremdet“ und sie als Ersatz für einen Serviettenring gewählt. Der Mix der Farben passt schön zusammen. Die Kerzen in Pink zaubern ein wunderbares Licht.

The pink of the napkins, vases, and candleholders is reflected in the large dinner plate and harmonizes with the gold.

The napkin rings are actually silk bracelets made from Hermès scarves. The mix of colors goes together beautifully. The candles in pink conjure up a wonderful light.

tip Light

Die Ausleuchtung des Tisches hat erheblichen Einfluss auf die Atmosphäre und die Stimmung am Tisch. Das Licht darf nicht zu grell sein, aber auch keinesfalls zu dunkel. Denn man sollte sehen, was auf dem Teller drapiert ist. Meistens dimme ich die Deckenleuchte und stelle zusätzlich viele Kerzen auf dem Tisch auf oder manchmal auch kleine Lampen, die elektrisch aufgeladen werden können. An der Seite brennt auch immer eine Tischleuchte auf einer Anrichte.

The lighting of the table has a considerable influence on the atmosphere and mood. The light should not be too bright, but also not too dark. After all, you should be able to see what is draped on the plate. I usually dim the ceiling light and additionally place many candles on the table or sometimes small lamps that can be charged electrically. There is also always a table lamp burning on a sideboard.

Warhol meets Meissen

Eine sehr progressive und ungewöhnliche Mischung von Porzellan. Vor Jahren habe ich diese Warhol Teller in New York gesehen, aber sie waren nicht käuflich zu erwerben. Ein paar Jahre später habe ich sie dann in einem Museumsshop in Washington wiederentdeckt und dann quer durch Amerika geschleppt, bevor sie zum Glück heil zu Hause gelandet sind. Inzwischen habe ich sie aber auch schon in Europa gesehen.

Warum nicht etwas Hypermodernes mit etwas sehr Traditionellem kombinieren? Die Gegensätze sind groß, aber der Mix macht es zu etwas Besonderem.

Die Pop-Art-Vorspeisenteller habe ich auf das weltbekannte „Indisch Purpur" von Meissen und auf auberginefarbenen Tischsets platziert. Zu der „schrägen" Kombination passt auch das schräggelegte Besteck. Pinkfarbene Gläser und Serviettenringe runden das Farbspiel ab.

A very progressive and unusual mix of porcelain. Years ago, I saw these Warhol plates in New York, but they were not available for purchase. A few years later, I rediscovered them at a museum store in Washington and then lugged them across the United States before they luckily made it home in one piece. In the meantime, I've seen them in Europe, too.

Why not combine something hypermodern with something extremely traditional? The contrasts are great, but the mix is what makes it special.

I paired the Pop Art appetizer plates with Meissen's world-famous "Indisch Purpur" atop eggplant-colored placemats. The quirky combination is emphasized by the slanted cutlery. Pink-colored glasses and napkin rings round out the play of colors.

Black dragons

Mein erstes Meissen Geschirr, den „Ming-Drachen“, habe ich mir gegönnt, nachdem ich 2008 meine Möbelfirma in Asien verkauft hatte. Es ist bis heute mein Lieblingsgeschirr. Es ist traditionell und handbemalt, aber durch die schlichte Form und den Drachen wirkt es sehr modern.

Immer öfter decke ich in kleiner Runde auch mal am Wohnzimmertisch. Es ist nicht so förmlich und die Atmosphäre etwas relaxter.

I treated myself to my first – quite expensive – Meissen tableware, the “Ming Dragon” after I sold my furniture company in Asia in 2008. To this day, it is still my favorite dinnerware. It is traditional and hand-painted, but the simple form and the dragon design give it a very modern feel.

Lately, I’ve been using my living room table to host smaller groups. It’s less formal and the atmosphere is more relaxed.

Numéro Couture

Dior table fashion

Um den Tisch mal wieder anders aussehen zu lassen, kaufe ich nicht immer ein komplettes Geschirr, sondern Einzelteile, die ich dann mit meinem bestehenden Geschirr mische.

Bei diesen Dior Vorspeisentellern hat mich das etwas blasse Blumen-/Vogelmotiv angesprochen. Nicht immer mag man es so farbenfroh. Auch diese Teller habe ich mit meinen Limoges Hauptspeisentellern kombiniert. Mal ohne Platzteller habe ich den Holztisch mit ockerfarbenen Tischsets gestaltet.

In order to give my table a new look, I don't always buy a complete set of new dishes, but rather I seek out individual pieces that I can mix with my existing dishes.

The slightly pale floral/bird motif of these Dior appetizer plates is what appealed to me. I don't always like my table settings to be so colorful. I also combined these plates with my Limoges dinner plates. This time, instead of charger plates, I used ocher-colored placemats on the wooden table.

Die kleinen Teller für Dips habe ich in meiner Sammlung von Herend gefunden. Sie passen sich den Farben des Vorspeisentellers an.

Die besonderen Blumen von Victor Breuer passen genau zu den Farben der Teller. Die gedrechselten Kerzen sehen sehr dekorativ aus. Das Blau findet sich ebenfalls im Teller wieder.

I found the small plates for dips in my collection from Herend. They match the colors of the appetizer plate.

The special flowers from Victor Breuer match the colors of the plates exactly. The turned candles look very decorative. The blue of the candles also matches the blue in the plates.

Pattern mix

A fall tablescape in gray, black, and red

Bei einem Stadtbummel habe ich diese witzigen Teller entdeckt. Nicht nur für Hundeliebhaber! Die Teller von John Derian & Astier de Villatte haben neben der Illustration einen besonderen Rand. Man kann es auf dem Foto nicht so genau sehen, aber das Design lebt ein wenig von der Unvollkommenheit. Denn die Farbe der Teller ist nicht überall gleich dick aufgetragen.

During a stroll through the city, I discovered these charming plates. Not just for dog lovers! These John Derian & Astier de Villatte plates have a special edge next to the illustration. You cannot see it so well in the photo, but the paint on the plates is not uniformly thick – and this imperfection is what makes them truly stand out.

Diese Teller habe ich auf dem Hermès Geschirr aus der Serie „Balcon du Guadalquivir" platziert und mit verschiedenen Fornasetti Tellern kombiniert.
Die Kombination in Grau-, Schwarz- und Rottönen wirkt harmonisch. Dazu passen gut die Hortensien und Blumen in dunklem und knalligem Rot sowie die roten Trinkgläser von Lambert. Die Tischläufer sind im Toile-de-Jouy-Muster.

I arranged these plates with the Hermès tableware from the "Balcon du Guadalquivir" series and combined them with various Fornasetti plates.
The combination of shades of gray, black, and red gives the table a harmonious appearance. It goes well with the hydrangeas and flowers in dark and bright red, as well as the red drinking glasses from Lambert. The table runners feature a Toile-de-Jouy pattern.

Catch of the day

OPULENCE THROUGH COLOR

So einen schlicht gedeckten Tisch ohne Tischwäsche findet man bei mir selten. Opulenz kann man aber auch durch einen Farbmix herbeiführen. Türkis, Flieder, Lila und Kobaltblau. Ein modernes Festival und Revival der Farben.

Das Geschirr von Reichenbach Fish & Flower hat Retro-Charme und erinnert an die Farbwelt der 6oer Jahre. Weiße Fische auf farbigem Grund wie auf den Tellern und farbige Fische auf weißem Grund wie auf den Tassen machen das Geschirr interessant.

Such a simple table without table linen is rarely found in my house. But opulence can also be expressed through mix of colors. Turquoise, lilac, purple, and cobalt blue. A modern festival and revival of colors.

The Reichenbach Fish & Flower dinnerware has retro charm and is reminiscent of the color scheme of the 60s. The white fish on a colored background on the plates and the colored fish on a white background on the cups make the dinnerware interesting.

Zu dem farbigen Geschirr habe ich mich aufgrund des Goldrands für ein goldenes Besteck entschieden. Das wirkt harmonischer. In meiner Sammlung habe ich auch farblich passende Gläser in Türkis und Pink gefunden, die den Tisch zusätzlich beleben.

Blumenarrangement mit Lila in farblich passenden Vasen. Diese dekorativen Vasen benötigen eigentlich keine Blumen. Das Trio sieht auch ohne umwerfend aus.

To go with the colorful dinnerware, I opted for gold flatware because of the gold rim on the plates – it looks more harmonious. In my collection, I also found matching glasses in turquoise and pink, which further enliven the table.

Flower arrangement with pops of purple in matching vases. These decorative vases don't even really need flowers – the trio also looks stunning without them.

A modular aesthetic HOW I LOVE IT

Ich mag die Serie DATUM von Fürstenberg auch deshalb, weil sie eine ultramoderne und klare Designsprache mit einer außergewöhnlichen Funktionalität vereint. Außergewöhnlich praktisch ist auch, dass alle Teile miteinander stapelfähig sind und somit auch zeitgemäß im Sinne der Nachhaltigkeit.

One of the reasons why I like the "DATUM" collection by Fürstenberg is because it combines an ultra-modern and clear design language with exceptional functionality. Another highly practical feature is that all the pieces can be stacked together and are therefore also contemporary in terms of sustainability.

tip Music

Mein Mann hat für Einladungen bei uns zu Hause eine spezielle Playlist erstellt, die er immer gerne abspielt. Das hängt natürlich vom Musikgeschmack ab und darf auch mal etwas provokativ sein, wenn es die Unterhaltung nicht völlig stört. Mit ruhiger Hintergrundmusik macht man allerdings selten etwas falsch. Man kann auch die Dekoration, das Essen und die Musik speziell aufeinander abstimmen, etwa kürzlich an einem „rumänischen Abend“ (die Vorfahren meines Manns kommen aus Siebenbürgen) mit rumänischen Spezialitäten (aus dem Kochbuch Carparti), rumänischer Tischdeko und rumänischer Folkloremusik.

My husband has created a special playlist for invitations at our house, which he always likes to play. Of course, this depends on his taste in music and can sometimes be a little provocative if it doesn't completely disrupt the conversation. However, you can rarely go wrong with quiet background music by Miles Davis, for example. You can also coordinate the decoration, the food and the music, for example recently at a „Romanian evening“ (my husband's ancestors come from Transylvania) with Romanian specialities (from the Carparti cookbook), Romanian table decorations and Romanian folklore music.

In meiner Porzellansammlung ist dieses cleane Geschirr-Design eine wirkliche Ausnahme. Vor allem in stressigen Phasen mag ich ruhige und klare Linien. Dem Design angepasst, habe ich das Geschirr auf einem blanken Holztisch gedeckt.

Das schwarze Besteck unterstreich die zeitlose Modernität. Die getrocknete Hortensie bringt einen schönen atmosphärischen Kontrast.

In my porcelain collection, this clean tableware design is a real exception. In stressful phases in particular, I like calm and clear lines. In keeping with the design, I arranged the tableware on wa blank wooden table.

The black cutlery underlines the timeless modernity, while the dried hydrangea adds a nice atmospheric contrast.

WINTER
SETTINGS

The Advent Tables

Modern yet rustic

Nicht jeder mag es opulent oder es steht der Sinn nach etwas anderem. Das rot-weiße Geschirr Balcon du Guadalquivir von Hermès mag ich ganz besonders zur Weihnachtszeit und benutze es im Dezember jeden Tag.

Der Adventskranz, ein paar Granatäpfel und Tannenzapfen reichen als Blumendekoration.

Die schlichten, grauen Servietten habe ich zum Dreieck gefaltet. Jeder Gast bekommt als süße Deko ein Weihnachtsplätzchen auf den Teller gelegt.

Das schwarze Besteck macht den Weihnachtslook modern.

Opulence isn't everyone's taste, and sometimes the occasion calls for something different. I particularly like red-and-white "Balcon Du Guadalquivir" tableware from Hermès at Christmastime, and I use it every day in December.

The Advent wreath, a few pomegranates and pine cones serve as floral decorations.

I folded the plain gray napkins into a triangle. Each guest gets a Christmas cookie on their plate as a sweet decoration.

The black cutlery gives this Christmas look a modern touch.

PPD

Christmas Couture

Weihnachten ganz klassisch, edel und schick. Dazu decke ich auf einer weißen Tischdecke das Porzellan „Taste“ von Reichenbach. Als Vorspeisenteller kombiniere ich die rot-weißen Teller von Dior aus der Serie “Toile de Jouy”, die ich in St. Tropez in der Dior Villa entdeckt habe. Durch das Dekor wirken sie ein bisschen exotisch.

Dazu passen ein konventionelles Silberbesteck und schlichte Weingläser am besten. Einen guten Kontrast bilden die schwarzen Wassergläser von Rotter Glas.

Ein Meer von weißen, unterschiedlichen Blumen passt am besten dazu und macht die Tischdekoration edel. Die Tannenzapfen machen den Look winter- und weihnachtlich.

A Christmas table that is classic, elegant, and chic. Here, I arranged the “Taste” porcelain collection from Reichenbach on a white tablecloth. As appetizer plates, I combined red-and-white Dior plates from the “Toile de Jouy” series, which I discovered in St. Tropez at the Dior Villa. The decor makes them look a bit exotic.

Conventional silver cutlery and plain wine glasses go best with these plates, while the black water glasses from Rotter Glas provide a nice contrast.

A sea of different white flowers is the best option here, lending the table a touch of class. The pine cones add a wintry feel that is perfect for Christmas.

Weihnachten darf es richtig opulent und von mir aus auch kitschig sein. Mehr ist in diesem Fall mehr!

Ich hole mein Weihnachtsgeschirr von Royal Copenhagen aus dem Schrank. Girlanden, Schleifen, Glocken. Weihnachtlicher kann es nicht sein.

Dazu kombiniere ich mein Silberbesteck sowie schlichte Weingläser und die schwarzen Drachengläser von Rotter Glas.

For me, Christmas is a time for opulence and even a bit of kitsch. In this case, more is more!

I get my Christmas dishes from Royal Copenhagen out of the cupboard. Garlands, bows, bells. Christmas is here!

I combine these dishes and decorations with my silver cutlery as well as plain wine glasses and the black dragon glasses from Rotter Glas.

Opulent Christmas

tip Flower decoration tips

Blumen kaufe ich schon immer einige Tage vor der Einladung oder frage den Blumenhändler, ob er schon Blumen mit geöffneten Blüten vorrätig hat. Denn Blumen schmücken den Tisch am schönsten, wenn sie in voller Blüte stehen.

I always buy flowers a few days before the invitation or ask the florist if he already has flowers with open blossoms in stock. Because flowers decorate the table most beautifully when they are in full bloom.

Für die prunkvolle Blumendekoration hat der Florist Victor Breuer gesorgt. Zwei große Kränze in der Mitte sind der Blickfang. Granatäpfel, Tannenzapfen, kleine Vasen in Gold mit roten Rosen und Orchideen. Ein Fest für die Sinne.

Die Kerzen von Engels Kerzen in unterschiedlichen Höhe und Stärken tauchen den Tisch in ein warmes, stimmungsvolles und festliches Licht. Ganz so opulent muss es vielleicht nicht sein, aber ein paar schöne Anregungen findest du bestimmt!

Florist Victor Breuer provided these magnificent floral decorations. Two large wreaths in the center are eye-catchers. Pomegranates, pine cones, small vases in gold with red roses and orchids. A feast for the senses.

The candles frcm Engels Kerzen in different heights and sizes bathe the table in a warm, atmospheric, and festive light. Maybe your table doesn't have to be quite so opulent, but you're sure to find a few beautif.l ideas!

NEW YORK
FÜR DIE HOSENTASCHE
JULIANE PIEPER

FINE
HAND CUT
CRYSTAL

tip Important

Es ist mir schon einige Mal passiert, dass ich bei Gästen, die ich noch nicht so gut kannte, vergessen habe zu fragen, ob jemand Vegetarier, vegan ist oder eine Allergie hat. Es gibt nichts Schrecklicheres, wenn der Gast dort sitzt und nur in der Beilage herumpikst. Das macht gleich eine komische Stimmung.

It happened to me a few times in the past that I forgot to ask guests I didn't know very well if they were vegetarian, vegan or had an allergy. There's nothing worse when the guest sits there and only picks at the side dish. It immediately creates a „funny" atmosphere when a guest doesn't feel comfortable and the host feels guilty.

Simple and classic

Wenn es immer näher auf Weihnachten zugeht, überlege ich mir voller Vorfreude, wie ich einen schönen Tisch für das Weihnachtsessen decken kann. Bei diesem Setting ist alles dabei: Opulenz, Schlichtheit und Klassik.

Als Basis dient dazu das Service „Fine Lines“ aus der Linie „Fluen“ der Porzellanmanufaktur Fürstenberg. Eine sehr moderne und dennoch klassische Variante eines Porzellans. Die dezente Farbgestaltung in Taupe gibt dem Service den edlen Charakter und ermöglicht gute Kombinationsvarianten. Egal ob zu Weihnachten oder im Hochsommer: ein Geschirr, das zu jeder Jahreszeit passt.

As it gets closer to Christmas, I get excited thinking about how I will set a beautiful table for Christmas dinner. This setting has it all: opulence, simplicity, and elegance.

The “Fine Lines” services from Fürstenberg’s “Fluen” collection serves as the basis for the table – a very modern yet timeless porcelain tableware. The subtle color scheme in taupe gives the service a regal feel and makes it easy to combine. Whether for Christmas or at the height of summer, it’s a tableware that suits every season.

In der Weihnachtszeit liebe ich eine ganz besondere Tischdekoration. Ein Hingucker ist die goldene Schleife, die um den Vorspeisenteller gebunden ist. Die Stoffservietten passen farblich perfekt zu der Kombination und heben die Schleifen nochmal hervor.

Dazu decke ich mein Silberbesteck und schlichte Weingläser. Als Wassergläser wähle ich wie so oft die schwarzen Gläser von Rotter Glas mit dem eingravierten Drachen. Sie sind modern und lockern das Bild ein wenig auf.

I love very special table decorations at Christmasttime. The golden bow tied around the starter plate is an eye-catcher. The color of the cloth napkins matches the combination perfectly and accentuates the bows.

I used my silver cutlery and simple wine glasses here. As so often, I choose the black glasses from Rotter Glas with the engraved dragon for the water glasses. They are modern and add a touch of relaxed charm.

A classy Christmas table in white, gold, and taupe

Ein festlich gedeckter Tisch in Weiß und Gold! Im Mittelpunkt des Tisches steht eine große, handgefertigte Lalique Kristallvase mit Amaryllis-Blumen und in Gold eingefärbten Blättern, die der Blickfang des Tisches ist.

A festive table set in white and gold! In the center of the table, I have placed a large, handmade Lalique crystal vase filled with amaryllis and gold-colored leaves that serves as the eye-catcher.

Do you already have ideas? ...

Ich habe meine geliebte taupefarbene Leinentischdecke gewählt, auf der weißes Geschirr besonders gut zur Geltung kommt. Neben der Vase liegen Äpfel und Tannenzapfen im Naturfarbton. Weiße Blumen und Christrosen in kleinen Vasen schmücken den Tisch zusätzlich. Das geschliffene Trinkglas in Schwarz bildet einen guten Kontrast. Ich habe mein ältestes Geschirr von Limoges auf einem weißen Platzteller von Reichenbach platziert. Das goldene Besteck passt wunderbar zu dem goldenen Porzellanrand.

I chose my beloved taupe linen tablecloth, which particularly complements white dishes. Next to the vase are apples and pine cones in a natural shade. White flowers and Christmas roses in small vases also decorate the table. The hand-cut drinking glass in black makes a good contrast. I arranged my oldest Limoges dinnerware on a white charger plate from Reichenbach. The gold flatware goes beautifully with the gold porcelain rim.

tip table runners and napkins

Hellgraue oder taupefarbene Tischläufer und Servietten sind eine gute Investition. Sie geben jedem Porzellan, auch wenn es noch so altmodisch gemustert ist, eine gewisse Modernität, Strenge und Klarheit. Aber auch zu weißem, schlichtem Porzellan sehen diese Farben phantastisch aus. Nicht nur zu Weihnachten!

Light gray or taupe table runners and napkins are a good investment. They give any porcelain rigor and clarity, no matter how old-fashioned the pattern may be.. But these colors also look fantastic with plain white china. Not just for Christmas!

When Athena came to Christmas

Weihnachten darf es richtig opulent sein! Die ausgeprägten Goldverzierungen des Geschirrs Grecque Athena aus der Porzellanmanufaktur Fürstenberg sind von Hand aufgetragen. Auf einem weißen Tischtuch wirkt es besonders festlich.

Christmas is the season for opulence! The distinctive gold decorations of the "Grecque Athena" dinnerware from Fürstenberg are applied by hand. These dishes look particularly festive on a white tablecloth.

Um dem traditionellen Design von 1840 eine moderne Interpretation zu geben, habe ich es auf einem Holztisch ohne Tischwäsche gedeckt. Auch die Weihnachtsdeko habe ich dazu schlicht gehalten und auf dem Tisch nur Strohsterne, Tannenzweige und ein paar goldene Kugeln dekoriert. Ich liebe die Kombination von traditionell und modern; opulent und schlicht. Das Schmuckstück auf dem Tisch ist zweifelsohne die Terrine!

To give the traditional design from 1840 a modern interpretation, I arranged it on a wooden table with no table linen. I also kept the Christmas decorations simple and only decorated the table with straw stars, fir branches, and a few golden baubles. I love the combination of traditional and modern, opulent and simple. The crown jewel of the table is undoubtedly the tureen!

Sylvester in schwarz-weiß. Mein Fornasetti Geschirr mit den unterschiedlich gestalteten Rändern habe ich auf einer weißen Decke, die in sich gemustert ist, platziert.

Für die Dekoration habe ich mir Perlenketten, Federn und Masken ausgedacht und diese auf dem Tisch verteilt. Ein bisschen Gatsby …

Zur Feier des Tages gibt es eine Menükarte, die ich farblich passend in Schwarz-Weiß und Gold gedruckt habe.

New Year's Eve in black and white. I arranged my Fornasetti tableware with the differently designed edges atop a patterned white tablecloth.

For the decoration, I found some beaded necklaces, feathers, and masks and spread them on the table. A hint of Gatsby ...

To mark the occasion, I also had a menu card printed in matching black, white, and gold.

Happy New Year in black and white

A homey breakfast

Auch ein Frühstück kann edel sein. Nicht immer hat man Gäste zu Hause. Auch wenn es morgens schnell gehen muss, decke ich den Tisch auf meinen Lieblingssets für den Herbst mit schönem Geschirr.

A quick breakfast can also be classy. You don't always have guests visiting. But even on busy mornings, I like to set the table with one of my favorite porcelain sets for fall.

Natürlich dekoriere ich zum Frühstück den Tisch nicht immer so aufwendig. Aber wenn das Geschirr entsprechend dekorativ ist, zaubert man schnell eine besondere Atmosphäre.

Die Linie „Clair de Lune“ von der Porzellanmanufaktur Fürstenberg decke ich besonders gerne zur dunklen Jahreszeit. Übersetzt heißt sie „Mondlicht“. Da es jetzt morgens wieder so spät hell und abends wieder so früh dunkel wird, passt das Geschirr perfekt in diese Zeit.

Of course, I don‘t always decorate the table so elaborately for breakfast. But when the tableware is this lovely, it creates a wonderful atmosphere.

I particularly like to set the "Clair de Lune" collection from Fürstenberg during the darker months of the year. „Claire de lune" translates to moonlight, and since it gets light so late in the morning and dark so early in the evening, theses tableware is perfect for this time of year.

Schäuble für europäisches Asylrecht

Die Form ist modern. Der Mustermix und auch die Oberfläche machen dieses Geschirr sehr lebendig. Es ist außergewöhnlich und dennoch vielseitig kombinierbar. Ganz besonders mag ich das Design der Kanne. Es ist ein richtiger Hingucker und ich erfreue mich jeden Morgen daran.

Mit den Tischsets aus Fell in Kombination ist die Stimmung gemütlich und trotzdem wirkt es modern.

The design is modern. The mix of patterns and the surface make this tableware very lively. It is unusual and yet can be combined in many ways. I particularly like the design of the coffee pot. It's a real eye-catcher and it brings me joy every morning.

The combination of the fuzzy placemats creates a cozy yet modern atmosphere.

Fashion dinner

Lust auf ein Dinner mit Anna Wintour? Eine modische Tischdekoration für ein Abendessen oder einen Lunch. Die Modewochen haben mich inspiriert, den Tisch „modisch“ zu decken.

Bei einem meiner letzten Museumsbesuche habe ich die Holzpuppen von Lucie Kaas entdeckt und finde, dass sie sich perfekt für eine außergewöhnliche Tischdekoration eignen. Hätte nicht jede modebewusste Frau gerne einmal mit Audrey Hepburn, Karl Lagerfeld oder Jackie O „geluncht“?

Fancy a dinner with Anna Wintour? This is a fashionable table setting for a dinner or lunch. The Fashion Weeks has inspired me to create a fashion-filled tablescape.

On one of my recent museum visits, I discovered Lucie Kaas‘ wooden dolls and think they are perfect for an unusual table setting. Wouldn‘t every fashion-conscious woman love to be able to have lunch with Audrey Hepburn, Karl Lagerfeld, or Jackie O?

tip Motto

Auch ein kleines Abendessen kann man unter ein Motto stellen. Dann fällt die Wahl der Deko leichter und es macht richtig Spaß, sich auf dem Themengebiet auszutoben. Die Gäste sind gespannt auf den Abend, haben sich selbst schon mit ihrem Look Mühe gegeben und „das Eis“ ist auch bei Gästen, die sich noch nicht kennen, schnell gebrochen.

A small dinner can also have a theme. Then it is easier to choose the decoration, it is really fun to let off steam in the theme area, the guests are excited about the evening, they have already made an effort with their look and „the ice“ is quickly broken even with guests who do not yet know each other.

Weiße Tischdecken lege ich selten auf, aber der Kontrast mit Schwarz, Rosa und Pink ist besonders schön. Ich habe mein altes Meissen „Indisch Purpur“ Porzellan mit modernen Fashion-Tellern kombiniert und auf den weißen Platztellern von Reichenbach platziert. Die schwarzen, handgeschliffenen Wassergläser von Rotter Glas passen gut zu den Holzfiguren.

I rarely use white tablecloths, but the contrast with the black, pink, and magenta is particularly beautiful. I combined my vintage Meissen "Indisch Purpur" china with modern fashion plates and placed them on white placemats from Reichenbach. The black hand-cut water glasses from Rotter Glas go well with the wooden figurines.

Kleine Vasen habe ich mit unterschiedlichen Blumen in Rosa und Pink bestückt.

Stumpenkerzen in Pink von Engels Kerzen ohne Kerzenständer und kleine Schalen mit Teelichtern habe ich überall auf dem Tisch verteilt. Farblich passende Macarons habe ich auch noch gefunden.

Stelle deinen Tisch doch unter ein Motto: mit Audrey Hepburn „Zum Frühstück bei …" oder „Ein Mittagessen mit Coco Chanel".

I filled small vases with a variety of flowers in pink and magenta.

I arranged pink pillar candles from Engels Kerzen without candlesticks and small bowls with tea lights around the table. I also found the perfect matching macarons ...

Give your table a theme, like "Breakfast at Tiffany's" with Audrey Hepburn or "A lunch with Coco Chanel."

Pink plus black & white

Eigentlich ein schlicht gedeckter Tisch, wenn nicht diese Farbexplosion stattfinden würde.

Auf einer taupe-farbenen Leinendecke von Gabriele Hofer habe ich Ginori Teller mit dem Platzteller von Fornasetti gedeckt. Ein Schwarz-Weiß-Mix. Die kleinen, goldenen Teller mit der schwarz-weißen Schlange von Jonathan Adler habe ich geschenkt bekommen. Sie lockern den Gesamteindruck edel auf.

Die pinkfarbenen Orchideen, auf verschiedene Wassergläser verteilt, machen diesen Tisch außergewöhnlich.

This would actually be quite a simple table setting if not for the explosion of color.

On a taupe linen tablecloth from Gabriele Hofer, I set Ginori plates with the charger plate from Fornasetti. A black-and-white mix. The small, golden plates with the black-and-white snake from Jonathan Adler were a gift. They lend a relaxed elegance to the overall table setting.

Several water glasses filled with pink orchids make it truly extraordinary.

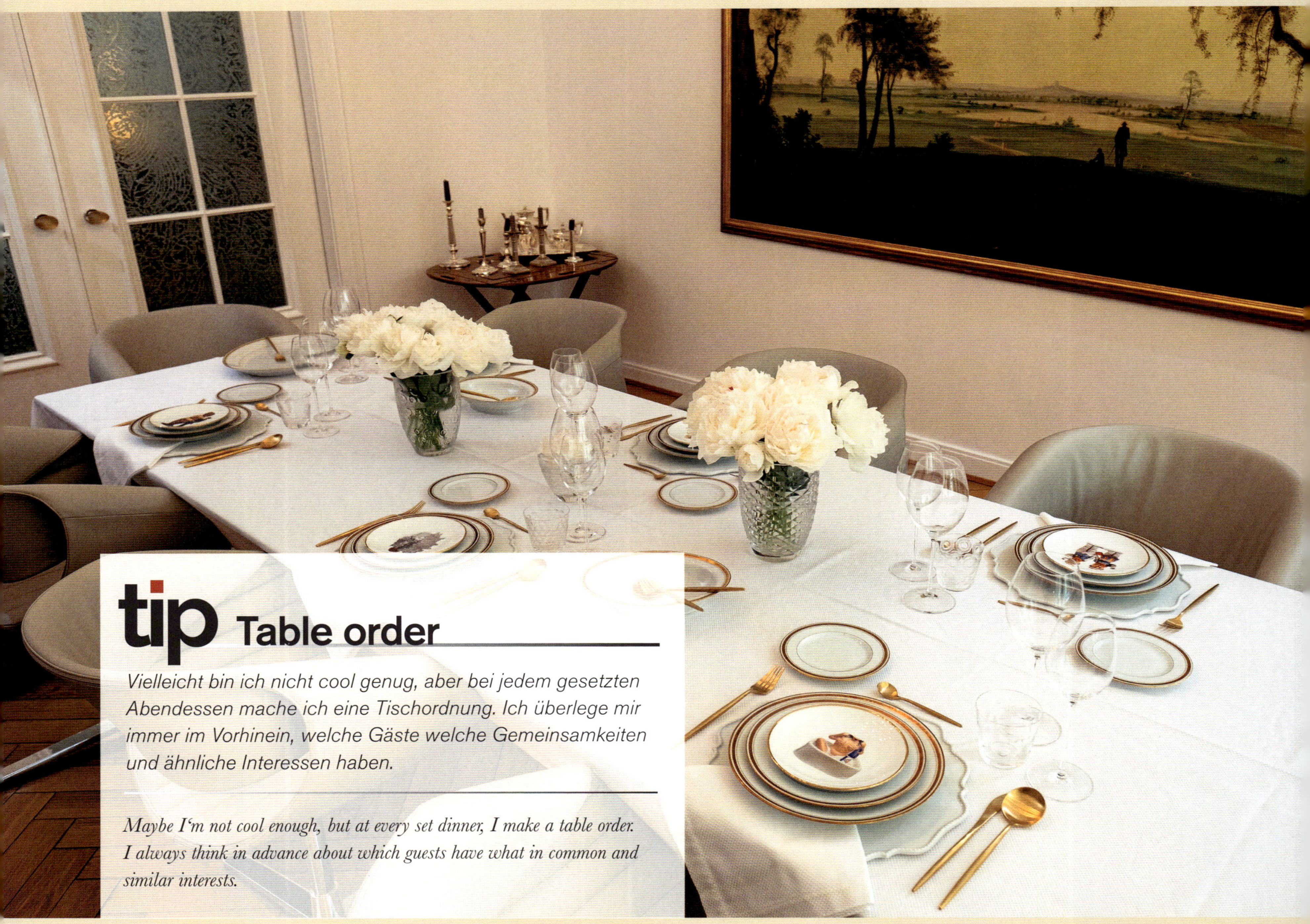

tip Table order

Vielleicht bin ich nicht cool genug, aber bei jedem gesetzten Abendessen mache ich eine Tischordnung. Ich überlege mir immer im Vorhinein, welche Gäste welche Gemeinsamkeiten und ähnliche Interessen haben.

Maybe I'm not cool enough, but at every set dinner, I make a table order. I always think in advance about which guests have what in common and similar interests.

Als ich bei einem New-York-Besuch im „L'Avenue at Saks", einem von Philippe Starck eingerichteten Restaurant, saß, konnte ich meine Augen nicht von diesem außergewöhnlichen Geschirr von Jeff Koons lassen. Mit klassischem Goldrand, aber super coolen Motiven. Ich liebe genau diese Gegensätze!

Sitting at a table at L'Avenue at Saks, a restaurant in New York designed by Philippe Starck, I could not take my eyes off this extraordinary tableware by Jeff Koons. A classic gold rim coupled with super cool motifs – these are the kinds of contrasts I love!

Koons meets Bernardaud

Der bekannte Künstler Jeff Koons hat das Service anlässlich des 150. Geburtstages des Hauses Bernardaud kreiert. Unter dem Namen „Banality Series“ hat der Künstler eine Kollektion von sechs unterschiedlichen Motiven geschaffen, bei denen er sich von verschiedenen Themen hat inspirieren lassen.

Um die Teller des Künstlers in den Vordergrund zu stellen, habe ich sie mit meinen schlichten Tellern von Limoges zusammen gedeckt.

Weil ich es schlicht halten möchte, wähle ich klassisch weiße Servietten, die ich zur Linken der Teller einmal im rechten Winkel gefaltet drapiert habe.

Famous artist Jeff Koons created this service for the 150th anniversary of the house of Bernardaud. Entitled “Banality Series,” the collection features six different motifs that were created by the artist and inspired by different themes.

To showcase the artist‘s plates, I combined them with my sleek Limoges plates.

Because I want to keep it simple, I chose classic white napkins, folded once at a right angle, that I draped in front of the plates.

Coziness

Gemütlich an grauen Tagen – und ein bisschen Farbe. „Fine Lines" von Fürstenberg kann man zu den unterschiedlichsten Anlässen decken, weil es sich durch die feinen, taupefarbenen Linien zu jeder Zeit anpasst.

Cozy on gray days – and a pop of color. "Fine Lines" by Fürstenberg can be used for a wide variety of occasions because its fine, taupe lines make it perfect for any occasion.

Als Basis dienen mir dazu meine taupefarbene Tischdecke und meine in Kombination gedeckten Tischläufer in einem dunklen Lila. Beides ist aus Leinen und stammt von Leitner (Gabriele Hofer). Das Farbkonzept zieht sich durch die gesamte Tischdekoration und lässt das Porzellan besonders gut herausstechen.

Die zur Tischdecke passenden Servietten unterbrechen die Farbe der Tischläufer und lassen diese noch besser hervorkommen.

The basis for this table setting is my taupe tablecloth combined with my dark-purple table runners. Both are made of linen and come from Leitner (Gabriele Hofer). The color concept is reflected throughout the entire table setting, allowing the porcelain to stand out particularly well.

The napkins, which match the tablecloth, break up the color of the table runners, making them stand out even more.

Aus Karneval mache ich mir nicht viel und am liebsten verreise ich zur 5. Jahreszeit. Aber wenn ich zu Hause bin, habe ich Spaß daran, den Tisch entsprechend zu decken. Bunte Farben machen gute Laune! Auf unterschiedlich bunten Platztellern decke ich mein Service von Limoges.

Ich möchte zwar einen Karnevalstisch decken, aber er soll gleichzeitig ein bisschen edel aussehen und so habe ich mal wieder eine weiße Tischdecke aus dem Schrank geholt, auf der die Farben besonders schön leuchten.

Passend zu dem Goldrand des Porzellans wähle ich mein Goldbesteck. Die grauen Stoffservietten lege ich diesmal eher „casual“ einfach auf den Teller und bestücke sie mit etwas Süßem.

Um es nicht zu bunt werden zu lassen, stelle ich schlichte Wasser- und Weingläser dazu. So liegt der Fokus auf dem Gedeck mit den farblich unterschiedlichen Platztellern.

I don't usually celebrate Carnival – in fact, I generally prefer traveling in order to avoid the festivities – but when I'm home, I have fun setting the table accordingly. Bright colors always lighten up the mood! For this setting, I combined my Limoges service with brightly colored charger plates.

I want to set a Carnival table, but at the same time, I want it to look classy. So, once again, I got my white tablecloth out from the closet because it truly lets the colors shine.

Matching the gold rim of the china, I chose my gold flatware. For this setting, I "casually" place folded gray napkins on the plates, topping them with a sweet treat.

To keep things from getting too colorful, I use simple water and wine glasses. This way, the focus is on the place setting with the different colored plates.

Funny Carnival

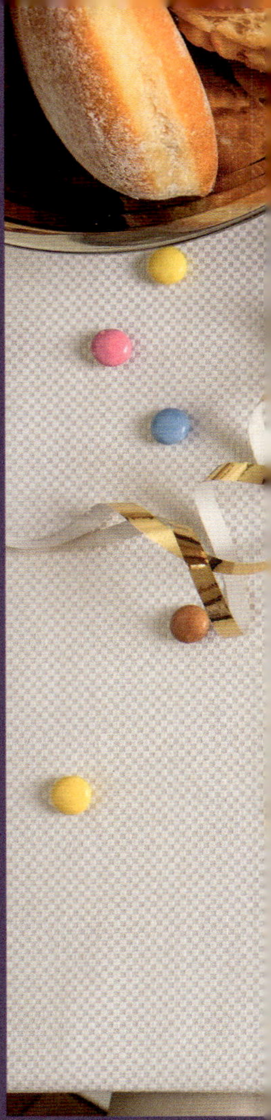
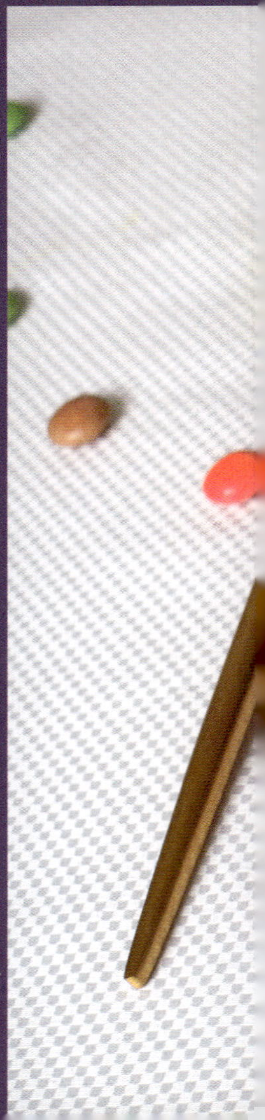

Mit Luftschlangen in Gold habe ich den Farbton vom Porzellan und dem Besteck aufgegriffen. Die glänzenden Luftschlangen wirken gleich edler.

Statt Konfetti verteile ich viele, bunte Smarties auf dem Tisch.

I used gold streamers to draw the eye to the hue of the porcelain and the cutlery. The shiny streamers immediately look more elegant.

Instead of confetti, I spread lots of colorful Smarties on the table.

A wild mix

The BIGGEST Mix and Match. Nicht jeder mag es, aber für mich ist es die Königsdisziplin an Kreativität. Es ist nicht nur opulent, sondern auch wild. Aber am Ende passt doch alles zusammen.

Der Reiche Drache von Meissen ist ohnehin schon ein auffälliges Dekor. Ich habe aber auch noch alle Farben abwechselnd gedeckt, und zwar auf bunten Tischläufern, die die Farben des Dekors beinhalten.

Um einen Kontrast zu bieten und den Tisch nicht altmodisch wirken zu lassen, habe ich die Platzteller von Gabriele Hofer mit einem Leopardenmotiv gewählt. Zu den bunten Blumen, die zum Läufer passen, habe ich wiederum schlichte Gläser gedeckt.

Einen weiteren Kontrast von traditionell und modern bildet die Beleuchtung: Silberleuchter neben den modernen Lampen von Kartell.

This is by far the BIGGEST mix and match. Not everyone likes it, but for me, it‘s the pinnacle of creativity. It‘s not only opulent, but also wild. And in the end, everything fits together.

The “Rich Dragon” design from Meissen is an eye-catching decor on its own. But I still made sure that the colors alternated and set the plates on colorful table runners that incorporate the the colors of the decor.

To provide contrast and keep the table from looking old-fashioned, I chose Gabriele Hofer‘s charger plates with a leopard-print motif. Once again, I chose plain glasses to go with the colorful flowers that match the runner.

Another contrast of traditional and modern is the lighting: silver candlesticksnext to the modern lamps from Kartell.

Picnic

Das sieht doch richtig nach Urlaub aus, oder? Picknick im Garten. Wenn man es sich schön macht, ist der Wohlfühleffekt überall.

Die Farben sind bunt gemixt und trotzdem schaut es harmonisch aus. Lila, Orange, Rosa, Blau, Grün. Alles geht. Gerade diese unterschiedlichen Farben machen es so lebendig.

Das Geschirr ist von Jars Céramistes, und für ein Essen unter freiem Himmel ist es besonders schön, weil es etwas rustikaler ist. Die Teller sind in Orange und Lila. Die Schalen sind gemustert.

This really looks like a vacation, doesn't it? Picnic in the garden. When you make it beautiful, it's guaranteed to make you feel great.

The colors are mixed and yet it looks harmonious. Purple, orange, pink, blue, green. Anything goes ... It's these different colors that make it so vibrant.

The tableware is from Jars Céramistes and it is especially nice for an outdoor meal because it is a bit more rustic. The plates are orange and purple. The bowls are patterned.

SPRING SETTINGS

The blankets and pillows also feature a colorful mix of patterns. Almost everything is from Missoni Home by Gabriele Hofer.

The blanket is quilted and therefore soft and comfortable when you lie on it. The colors of the different pillows blend wonderfully. The flowers also match the color scheme. The placemats and napkins are from Le Jacquard Français, also by Gabriele Hofer.

I especially love this table linen for dining outside in the summer because the texture is a bit thicker. The colors are intense and summery.

The large lanterns conjure up a special atmosphere in the evening with burning candles. And, of course, my outfit has to match as well ...

Bunter Mustermix auch bei den Decken und Kissen. Fast alles ist von Missoni Home von Gabriele Hofer.

Das Plaid ist wattiert und daher weich und bequem, wenn man darauf liegt. Die Farben der verschiedenen Kissen fügen sich wunderbar zusammen.

Die Blumen passen sich ebenfalls der Farbwelt an. Die Sets und Servietten sind von Le Jacquard Français, auch von Gabriele Hofer. Ich liebe diese Tischwäsche besonders im Sommer für draußen, weil die Textur etwas dicker ist. Die Farben sind intensiv und sommerlich.

Die großen Windlichter zaubern am Abend mit brennenden Kerzen eine besondere Atmosphäre. Natürlich muss dann auch noch mein Outfit farblich passen.

Bringing spring to the Table

Auch wenn der Frühling erst langsam in Fahrt kommt, kann man es auf dem Tisch schon frühlingshaft werden lassen. Die Kombination von Pink und Grün mag ich besonders gerne. Ich habe gestöbert und verschiedene Porzellane miteinander kombiniert.

Die Vorspeisen- und Essteller sind von Ginori. Der pinkfarbene Teller mit den Blättern ist von La DoubleJ. Die kleinen Teller sind von Jonathan Adler. Dazu habe ich noch einige Teller von Meissen aus der Serie Reicher Drache kombiniert. Von Reichenbach sind die weißen Platzteller.

Even if spring is only just starting, you can already bring the springtime spirit to your table. I particularly like the combination of pink and green. I have rummaged in my collection and combined different porcelains with one another.

The appetizer plate and dinner plate are from Ginori. The pink plate with the leaves is from La DoubleJ. The small plates are from Jonathan Adler. I also combined a few plates from Meissen from the "Rich Dragon"series. The white plates are from Reichenbach.

Die Teller in Grün und Pink habe ich abwechselnd in umgekehrter Farbkombi aufeinandergestellt. Die Blumendeko von Victor Breuer ist ein fröhlicher Mix aus Pink- und Rosatönen mit ein wenig Weiß. Das Weiß nimmt die Farbe der Platzteller wieder auf.

Mein Outfit passt sich farblich dieses Mal nicht der Dekoration an. Aber die Sonne darf auch am Tisch scheinen ...

I alternated the green and pink plates, with different colors on top and bottom at each place. The floral decor from Victor Breuer is a cheerful mix of pinks and fuschia with a little white, which picks up the color of the place settings.

This time my outfit doesn‘t match the color of the decor, but the sun may also shine at the table ...

Shades of Pink

Farbspiel in Pink. Tradition trifft italienischen Chic. Ein Spagat zwischen Opulenz und modernem Lifestyle.

A play of colors in pink. Tradition meets Italian chic. A balancing act between opulence and modern lifestyle.

Die Schüsseln von Meissen aus der Serie „Indisch Purpur“ und das Dekor „Reicher Drache“ (ebenfalls von Meissen) passen wunderbar zu dem italienischen Geschirr von Ginori.

Die Servietten, die Blumendeko und die Gläser habe ich alle in Pink gewählt.

The bowls from Meissen's “Indisch Purpur” collection and the plates from the “Rich Dragon” collection (which is also from Meissen) fit wonderfully with the Italian tableware Ginori.

I chose napkins, flowers, and glasses that are all different shades of pink.

Joyful Easter

Auch zu Ostern kommt unser altes Meissen Porzellan „Indisch Purpur“ in Pink auf den Tisch. Ich decke es im Frühling und Sommer am liebsten. Dieses Mal kombiniert mit Grün und einer Prise Türkis.

Once again for Easter, the table is set with our trusty Meissen “Indisch Purpur” porcelain in pink. I love to set it in the spring and summer. This time, I combined it with green and a hint of turquoise.

Die Tischläufer und Sets in hellem Grün sind von Gabriele Hofer. Die Ostereier kariert. Die Gläser in Pink und Grün lassen das Gesamtbild moderner erscheinen.

Blumen dürfen auf der Ostertafel nicht fehlen. Die Windlichter habe ich als Vase „umfunktioniert". Victor Breuer hat mir zwei schöne Tischsträuße in Pink mit großen Rosen zusammengestellt.

Überall auf dem Tisch verteilt habe ich kleine Osterkörbchen mit Schokoladeneiern platziert.

Die farblich passenden Macarons schmecken nicht nur gut, sondern sehen auch immer optisch nett aus. Auf jedem Platz steht ein Schokoladenosterhase, der den Ostertisch noch sympathischer macht.

The table runners and placemats in light green are from Gabriele Hofer. I decorated the Easter eggs as a nest in a silver bowl. The glasses in pink and green make the overall look more modern.

Flowers are an absolute must for any Easter table. I "repurposed" the candleholders as vases. Victor Breuer put together two beautiful table bouquets in pink with large roses.

I placed small Easter baskets with chocolate eggs around the table.

The matching macarons not only taste good, but also look lovely as well. As another cute touch, a chocolate Easter bunny has been set at each place.

tip Give-aways

Damit sich die Gäste an das schöne Miteinander noch lange erinnern, kann man jedem Gast kleine Geschenke mitgeben, einen tollen Wein mit eigener Banderole, eine selbstgemachte Marmelade in einem schönen Glas oder ein selbstgebackenes Brot.

To make sure that the guests remember the beautiful togetherness for a long time, you can give each guest small gifts, a great wine with its own banderole, a homemade jam in a beautiful jar or a homemade loaf of bread.

Helles Gelb, gepaart mit Rosa, ist auch in der Mode eine schöne Kombination. Passend habe ich einen Ostertisch gedeckt und noch die Farbtöne Apricot und Pink addiert.

Das schlichte, weiße Geschirr mit dem Goldrand von Limoges begleitet mich schon seit 1996. Die Platzteller in Apricot wollte ich zwischenzeitlich schon mal entsorgen. Wie gut, dass ich sie doch behalten habe. Denn in Verbindung mit dem Tischläufer in Rosa wirkt es insgesamt frisch und frühlingshaft.

Die gelben Servietten haben mir zwischenzeitlich auch gar nicht mehr gefallen, aber zu dieser Tischdeko passen sie perfekt.

Light yellow paired with pink is also a beautiful combination in fashion. Fittingly, I set an Easter table and added the shades of apricot and pink.

I've had this sleek, white tableware set with a gold rim from Limoges since 1996. At one point, I wanted to throw away the apricot plates, but I'm happy I kept them because they look fresh and springy together with the table runners.

At some point I also fell out of love with the yellow napkins, but they're perfect for this table setting.

Spring is on the way

tip Place cards

Die Tischkarten beschrifte ich immer von beiden Seiten, so dass das Gegenüber sich den Namen nochmals schnell in Erinnerung rufen kann.

I always write on both sides of the place cards so that the other person can quickly remember the name.

Statt Tischkarten hat jeder ein Plätzchen mit seinem Namen auf dem jeweiligen Teller. Alle Naschereien und die Cupcakes habe ich in den passenden Farben ausgewählt und im bunten Mix auf die Etagere gelegt. Auch die Eier sind passend eingefärbt und auf dem Osterzopf drapiert. Natürlich sind auch die Streublumen farblich abgestimmt.

Die restliche Osterdekoration und die eierförmigen Kerzen von Engels sind in Naturfarben gehalten.

Die Windlichter in Altrosa mit Gold passen auch noch gut zur Tischdekoration. Die große Vase, ein Erbstück meiner Großeltern und die Karaffe in Gold bringen noch etwas Glamour auf den Tisch.

Instead of place cards, everyone gets a cookie printed with their name on their plate. I chose all the nibbles and the cupcakes in matching colors and placed them in a colorful mix on the étagère. The eggs are also dyed to match and arranged on top of the Easter bread. Of course, the scattered flowers are also color coordinated.

The rest of the Easter decorations and the egg-shaped candles from Engels are in natural colors.

The candleholders in antique pink with gold also go well with the table decorations. The large vase, an heirloom from my grandparents, and the carafe in gold add a touch of glamour to the table.

Happy
Easter

Sobald das Wetter es zulässt, decke ich draußen auf der Terrasse. Das „Indisch Purpur“ wirkt auf Grau ganz besonders edel! Um die Tischdekoration etwas außergewöhnlicher, aber dennoch klassisch wirken zu lassen, verwende ich zwei farblich unterschiedliche Tischläufer. Der eine Läufer ist grau und der andere ist rosa. Die Servietten in Grau machen den Look moderner.

Die gradlinigen Wassergläser in Pink lassen ein traditionelles Service moderner erscheinen. Altherkömmliche Service müssen nicht notwendigerweise altmodisch oder spießig aussehen. Wie in der Mode kommt es auf das Styling an!

As soon as the weather permits, I set the table outside on the terrace. My “Indisch Purpur” set looks particularly elegant on gray! To make the table decoration look a little more unusual but still classic, I used two different colored table runners. One runner is gray and the the look more modern.

The striped water glasses in pink make a traditional service look more modern. Old, traditional services don’t necessarily have to look old-fashioned or stuffy. Just like in fashion, it‘s all about how you style it!

Indian purple

Die kleinen Teller hat mir meine Schwiegermutter geschenkt. Sie sind von Taitu und passen sehr schön dazu.

Ich liebe die Form dieser Teekanne von Reichenbach. Sie passt zu jedem Service. Die Pfingstrosen passen besonders gut zu diesem Porzellan.

The small plates were given to me by my mother-in-law. They are from Taitu and match very nicely.

I love this shape of this teapot from Reichenbach. It goes well with any service. The peonies go especially well with this china.

Cosmopolitan

Wie immer! Der Mix macht's! So kann man jede Tischdekoration anders und originell gestalten.

Ein Meissen Cosmopolitan Teller mit einem Vorspeisenteller von Hermès Balcon du Guadalquivir im Mix. Obwohl die Muster der Porzellane sehr unterschiedlich sind, wirkt die Kombination trotzdem harmonisch und modern.

As usual, it's all about the mix! That's what lets you make any table setting unique and original.

A Meissen "Cosmopolitan" plate is combined with an appetizer plate from the Hermès "Balcon du Guadalquivir" collection. Although the patterns of the porcelains are very different, the combination still looks harmonious and modern.

Plage d'ALLUDE

Die Glasteller in Rot-Orange habe ich auch schon ewig und sie passen zufällig gut zu diesem Farbspiel. Die Platzteller in Türkis sind nichts Besonderes, aber passen ins Thema. Die Tischwäsche habe ich bei dem Mustermix und der Farbintensität weiß gehalten.

Die Serviette ist geknotet und liegt auf der Seite des Tellers. Für die Dekoration in der Mitte wähle ich noch einen Porzellan-Kakadu in schlichtem Weiß und ein paar blaue Hortensien.

I've also had the glass plates in red and orange forever, and they happen to go well with this color scheme. The placemats in turquoise are nothing special, but they fit the theme.

I kept the table linens white as a contrast to the bright colors and the crazy mix of patterns. The napkin is knotted and lies on the side of the plate. For the decoration in the middle, I chose a porcelain cockatoo in plain white and a few blue hydrangeas.

Wildlife on your plate

Das Geschirr Carnets d'Équateur von Hermès passt zu jeder Jahreszeit. Ich decke es tatsächlich gerne in verschiedensten Situationen. Der Goldrand macht das Porzellan elegant. Aufgelockert wird das Design durch die verschiedenen Motive der Teller. Wenn man keine Zeit hat, noch Blumen zu besorgen, kann man den Tisch auch mit Farn aus dem eigenen Garten dekorieren.

The "Carnets d'Équateur" dinnerware from Hermès is perfect for any season. I like to set it in a wide variety of situations. The gold rim makes the porcelain elegant. The design is broken up by the different motifs of the plates. If you don't have time to run out and get flowers, you can also decorate the table with ferns from your own garden.

Lange Zeit mochte ich gar keine Tischdecken mehr, aber irgendwie ändert sich immer der Geschmack von Zeit zu Zeit und nun mag ich es wieder etwas opulenter. Diese gelbe Tischdecke hat mein Mann mit „in die Ehe gebracht", wie man so schön sagt. Ich habe sie neulich bei der Suche nach anderen Dingen ganz unten im Schrank wiedergefunden und neu entdeckt. Denn mit dem eleganten Porzellan sieht sie gar nicht mehr so „rustikal" aus, wie ich es damals empfunden habe. Dem Geschirr gibt man in der Kombination etwas mehr Leichtigkeit.

For a long time, I no longer liked tablecloths, but somehow our tastes tend to change over time, and now I like things to be a bit more opulent again. My husband brought this yellow tablecloth "into the marriage," as they say. I found it the other day while I was looking for something else at the very bottom of my closet and rediscovered it. With the elegant porcelain, it no longer looks as "rustic" as I used to think it was. The combination also brings out the brightness of the dishes, making them pop.

Den „glucksenden Fisch“ kennst du bestimmt als Karaffe. In Gold ein richtiger Hingucker und passt zu jedem Geschirr.

Ich habe ihn als Vase umfunktioniert und passend in Gelb Sonnenblumen ausgesucht. Noch ein paar Zitronen dazu und fertig ist die Tischdekoration. Eine einfache und schlichte Deko, die trotzdem Aufmerksamkeit auf sich zieht.

Surely you're familiar with the "gurgling fish" jug. In gold, it's a real eye-catcher and matches every tableware.

Here I used it as a vase, filling it with the perfect yellow sunflowers. Add a few lemons to the table and voilà. A sleek, simple table decoration that still makes a statement.

Fairytale Colors

A COLORFULLY DECORATED TABLE

Farben wie im Märchen. Meine Lieblingssommerfarben vereint. Helles Lila mit Apfelgrün und Zitronengelb im Mix. Das Service „Colour“ von Reichenbach ist angelehnt an klassische Formen. Ich mag es auch Ton-in-Ton. Zum Beispiel in Orange oder Grau, aber im Sommer mag ich den Farbmix. Dieses Geschirr decke ich am liebsten zum Frühstück oder für Kaffee und Kuchen. Die Leinentischdecke von Gabriele Hofer nimmt die Farben auf. Witzig dazu die Kürbis- und KOIKOI-Vasen sowie die Serviettenringe. Farblich passende Macarons oder andere Süßigkeiten machen den Anblick harmonisch. Dazu habe ich schlichte Servietten gewählt.

Colors like in a fairy-tale. My favorite summer colors combined. A mix of light purple, apple green and lemon yellow. The “Colour” service from Reichenbach is inspired by classic shapes. I also like it when all the pieces are the same color, for example, in orange or gray, but in the summer, I like the mix of colors. I prefer to set this tableware for breakfast or for coffee and cake. The linen tablecloth from Gabriele Hofer matches the colors perfectly. The Pumpkin and KOIKOI vases as well as the napkin rings are charming accents. Matching macarons or other sweets balance the table decoration. For this table, I have chosen plain napkins.

SOMMER SETTINGS

Into the jungle

Auch farbenfroh kann edel aussehen. Hier habe ich nicht nur die Platzteller von Cavalli im Leolook, sondern auch die passenden Vorspeisen- bzw. Kuchenteller von Gabriele Hofer gedeckt. Der Essteller ist von Limoges.

Die Weingläser in Grün und die Wassergläser in Pink spiegeln die Farben der Sets wider. Bunte Blumen, ebenfalls in den Farben der Sets, und die Deko-Pfauen in Gold, die die Farbe des Bestecks aufnehmen, machen den Tisch trotz der Farbigkeit harmonisch und dekorativ.

Colorful can also be classy. Here I've used not only the Cavalli leopard-print charger plates, but also the matching appetizer and cake plates, respectively, from Gabriele Hofer. The dinner plate is from Limoges.

The wine glasses in green and the water glasses in pink mirror the colors of the placemats. Colorful flowers also in the colors of the placemats and the decorative gold peacock figurines, which mirror the color of the cutlery, make the table appear harmonious and decorative despite all the different colors.

The Taste

Tradition and modernity, perfectly combined

Dieses Geschirr von Reichenbach – „Taste“ von Paola Navone – ist ein sehr schönes „Basisgeschirr“ und lässt sich vielfältig einsetzen. Es ist durch seine unterschiedlich gestalteten Formen wunderschön und kombiniert Design, Tradition und Moderne. In Weiß passt es auf jeden Tisch und zu jeder Einrichtung. Ich nenne es „Basisgeschirr“, weil man es nicht nur so decken kann, sondern auch mit allen anderen Porzellanen mischen kann. Hier steht es auf einer orangefarbenen Tischdecke von Le Jacquard Français von Gabriele Hofer.

Die Gläser in Gelb, Pink und Orange machen das Erscheinungsbild fröhlich und sommerlich. Die kleinen, blütenförmigen Schalen in Rotgold bzw. Kupfer passen gut zu der Farbstimmung. Bei diesem Geschirr habe ich mich von Doris Zehr, einer Porzellansammlerin, inspirieren lassen.

This tableware – “Taste” by Paola Navone for Reichenbach – is a very nice basic tableware and can be used in many ways. Its differently designed shapes are what make it beautiful, and it combines design, tradition, and modernity. In white, it goes with every table and every interior. I call it basic dinnerware because you can not only use it as a complete set, but also mix and match it with other porcelain. Here, I’ve paired it with an orange tablecloth by Gabriele Hofer for Le Jacquard Français.

The glasses in yellow, pink, and orange make the look cheerful and summery. The small, flower-shaped bowls in rose gold or copper go well with the color mood. For this tableware, I was inspired by Doris Zehr, a porcelain collector.

VOGUE

CLASSIC PORCELAIN STYLISHLY STAGED

Klassisches Porzellan kann man auch sehr stylisch in Szene setzen. Es kommt auf die Accessoires an.

Als ich diesen Tisch gedeckt habe, war ich gerade inspiriert von der Fashion Week in Paris.
Das Porzellan von Reichenbach lässt unterschiedliche Interpretationen zu und sieht je nach Styling immer wieder ganz anders aus.

Classic porcelain can also be staged very stylishly. It all depends on the accessories.

When I set this table, I was just inspired by Paris Fashion Week.
Reichenbach porcelain allows for different interpretations and always looks completely different depending on the styling.

Verschiedene Titelblätter von Modemagazinen wie Vogue, Glamour, InStyle, Elle, Madame, Harper's Bazaar habe ich statt einer Decke auf dem Tisch verteilt. Durch die knalligen Farben kommt das weiße, schlichte Porzellan besonders gut zur Geltung. Die Cover ziehen die Aufmerksamkeit auf sich. Daher braucht es nicht viel mehr Deko. Nur eine kleine, weiße Rosenthal Vase, die ich schon ewig habe, ist mit einer pinkfarbenen Gerbera bestückt.

Ein kleiner weiterer Farbtupfer sind die farbigen Wassergläser. Dazu wähle ich für jeden Platz eine andere Farbe. Die Farben spiegeln sich in den Magazinen wider. Eine außergewöhnliche und spannende Tischdekoration, die ein echter Hingucker ist und die man ganz individuell gestalten kann.

Instead of a tablecloth, I spread the covers of various fashion magazines such as Vogue, Glamour, InStyle, Elle, Madame, and Harper's Bazaar over the table. The bright colors make the sleek, white porcelain stand out especially well. The covers draw attention to themselves. Therefore, the table does not need much more decoration. Only a small, white Rosenthal vase, which I have had forever, with a single pink gebera.

The colored water glasses offer another small splash of color. For this table, I choose a different color for each place setting. The colors are reflected in the magazines. An unusual and exciting table decoration that is a real eye-catcher and can be customized.

TAYLOR HILL
TE QUIERE COMO:
AMIGA
POLOLA
TOUCH AND GO
GIRL POWER!
Relaxed
Chic
moves
Consigan el ritmo perfecto en la cama
36+ BOLD PIECES TO BRIGHTEN UP YOUR STYLE
CAMBIO

Matching white and blue

Lange konnte ich blau-weiß gemustertes Porzellan nicht mehr sehen und plötzlich finde ich es wieder wunderschön. Ich habe das traditionelle Zwiebelmuster einmal ganz anders gedeckt und trotzdem sieht es immer noch klassisch aus, aber mit einer Prise Modernität. Denn ich habe es mit einem blau-weissen Hermès-Teller gemixt.

For a long time, I was sick and tired of blue-and-white patterned porcelain, but suddenly I find it beautiful again. Here, I've used the traditional Meissen "Blue Onion" pattern in an entirely new way, and yet it still looks classic, but with a hint of modernity. Because I matched it with a blue-white Hermès-Plate.

Trotz der beiden unterschiedlichen Blautöne kann man die Teller sehr gut miteinander kombinieren. Dieses Mal habe ich auch eine Sammlung blauer Römergläser dazu gedeckt, um die Farben noch einmal aufzugreifen. Auch wenn die Töne unterschiedlich sind, passt es gut zusammen.

Die Römergläser nutze ich als Wassergläser. Der Wein wird aus den feinstieligen Gläsern mit einer ganz besonderen Form von Zalto getrunken.

Even though they have two different shades of blue, the plates still look lovely together. This time, I also used a collection of blue Rummer-style glasses to once again mirror the colors. Even though the shades are different, they go well together.

I use the Rummer-style glasses as water glasses. The wine will be served in thinly stemmed glasses with a very special shape from Zalto.

Da Blau eine sehr kühle Farbe ist, habe ich mich dazu entschlossen, kein Silberbesteck zu wählen, sondern goldenes Besteck. Ein schöner Bruch, der die Kombination außergewöhnlicher aussehen lässt. Die Tischläufer sind hellgrau. Weiß kann schnell spießig wirken. Blau wäre zu viel. Das helle Grau macht das Erscheinungsbild moderner und trotzdem edel Unterschiedlich violette Blumen in ebenso unterschiedlichen Vasenformen runden das Bild ab.

Man muss nicht immer für mehrere Personen decken, um das gute Geschirr aus dem Schrank zu holen. Manchmal reicht es auch, einmal nur für zwei schön zu decken.

Since blue is a very cool color, I decided not to use silver cutlery, but rather gold cutlery. A nice break that makes the combination look even more unique. The table runners are light gray. White can quickly look stuffy. Blue would be too much. The light gray makes the look more modern yet classy. Different purple flowers in a variety of different vase shapes complete the picture.

You don't always need to host a lavish dinner party to get the good dishes out of the cupboard. Sometimes, it's enough to create a fabulous table for two.

When creativity runs wild

Bei sonnigem Wetter blühe ich auf und die Laune steigt. Ich bin voller Energie und Lebenslust. Geht es dir genauso? Und man kann seiner Kreativität freien Lauf lassen ...

Auf bunte Tischläufer setze ich zunächst die Platzteller im Leomuster von Gabriele Hofer. Das Leopardenmuster ist nicht nur in der Mode ein Dauerbrenner, sondern macht jeden gedeckten Tisch außergewöhnlich und es passt zu jeder Farbe. In der Mode sage ich: Leo geht immer!

Ich habe geschaut, welche Farben kommen in dem Tischläufer vor und welches Geschirr habe ich farblich passend dazu im Schrank.

Das gute alte Zwiebelmuster und blau-weiße Teller von Hermès finde ich in meinem Repertoire. Auch die Farben der Römergläser und der verschiedenen Blumen finden sich im Tischläufer wieder und so fügt es sich zu einem harmonischen Mix zusammen.

When the sun comes out, I come alive and I'm instantly happier. I am full of energy and joie de vivre. Do you feel the same way? And you can give your creativity free rein ...

On top of colorful table runners, I first used the leopard-print charging plates from Gabriele Hofer. The leopard-print pattern is not only a perennial favorite in fashion, but it makes every table setting extraordinary and it goes with every color. In fashion, I say: leopard-print pattern!

I looked at the colors in the table runner and what tableware I have in my closet in matching colors.

I found my good old Meissen "Blue Onion" porcelain as well as blue-and-white plates from Hermès in my repertoire. Also, the colors of the Rummer-style glasses and the various flowers can also be found in the table runner, all adding up to a harmonious mix.

Eine günstige Vase steht neben einer Meissen Vase. Das macht nichts, denn im Mix sieht der Gesamteindruck hochwertig aus. Das goldene Besteck macht den Look moderner, aber ein Silberbesteck würde auch gut passen.

Lass deiner Kreativität freien Lauf und probiere mal etwas Neues aus!

I've placed an inexpensive vase next to an expensive Meissen vase. It doesn't matter, because when combined, the overall impression is still chic and elegant. The gold cutlery makes the look more modern, but silver cutlery would also work well.

Let your creativity run wild and try something new!

An entirely new design vocabulary!

Weißes Gold mit Gold. „Vitruv“ von Meissen. Reduziert und klar ist dieser Tisch gedeckt. Auf eine weiße Tischdecke habe ich Fellsets gelegt. Sie machen den Look cooler und weniger elegant.

White and yellow gold. “Vitruv” by Meissen. This table setting is minimalist and clear. I used four placemats on a white tablecloth. They make the look cooler and less stuffy.

tip Hostess style

Als Gastgeberin ziehe ich mich immer weniger elegant an, als wenn ich selbst eingeladen bin. Einmal ist es mir ergangen, dass ich im Vergleich zu einem Paar völlig overdressed war. Oberstes Gebot: Der Gast soll sich wohlfühlen!

As a hostess, I always dress less elegantly than when I am invited myself. Once I was completely overdressed compared to a couple. The first commandment: the guest should feel comfortable!

Nur ein paar farbige Blumen und filigrane Porzellanfiguren schmücken den Tisch. Die fein geschliffenen Trinkgläser von Rotter Glas unterstreichen die edel gedeckte Tafel.

Only a few colorful flowers and delicate porcelain figurines decorate the table. The finely cut drinking glasses from Rotter Glas underline the elegantly set table.

Couture collage outside

Tradition modern interpretiert. Mix and Match. Die Porzellanserie „The Meissen Collage“ habe ich während eines Besuchs in Weimar vor ein paar Jahren zufällig entdeckt. Die Idee ist, das traditionelle Zwiebelmuster ganz neu und modern zu interpretieren. Alte Dekorelemente sind neu in Szene gesetzt.

Zu dieser Kollektion gehören verschiedene Serien, die auch alle wieder zueinander passen, obwohl sie sehr unterschiedlich sind.

A modern take on tradition. Mix and match. I discovered the porcelain series "The Meissen Collage" by chance during a visit to Weimar a few years ago. The idea is to interpret the traditional "Blue Onion" pattern in a completely new and modern way. Old decorative elements are reimagined.

This collection includes several series that all work with one another, even though they are all very different.

Prima! So passen auch meine kleinen Schalen mit dem herkömmlichen Zwiebelmuster perfekt dazu. Auch andere Porzellane kann man dazumischen.
Um den Mustermix nicht zu wild werden zu lassen, habe ich wieder schlichte Tischläufer in Taupe und zeitlose Weingläser von Riedel kombiniert.

Die geschliffenen Wassergläser sind von Rotter Glas. Das Besteck für den Dessert ist über Kreuz gelegt und erinnert an die Schwerter von Meissen. Die Serviette liegt lässig an der Seite.

Great! This means my small bowls with the traditional "Blue Onion" pattern also match perfectly. Other porcelains can also be combined with this setting. To keep the pattern mix from getting too wild, I once again plain table runners in taupe and timeless wine glasses from Riedel. The cut water glasses are from Rotter Glas.

The cutlery for dessert is crisscrossed and reminiscent of Meissen's crossed swords logo. The napkin is placed casually on the side.

Couture collage inside

Die geliebte Affenkapelle. Manche mögen sie spießig und altmodisch finden, aber ich liebe sie über alles! Das „Meissen Collage" habe ich mit der Affenkapelle kombiniert.

Damit es nicht verstaubt wirkt, platziere ich alles auf taupefarbenen Tischläufern. Als Blumen wähle ich Disteln. Sie wirken streng und machen den lieblichen Eindruck der Affenkapelle moderner. Hier passt das im Design moderne Besteck in Gold gut dazu.
Auch dies ist ein Bruch, ein Mix verschiedener Stilrichtungen, die eine Tischdekoration interessant machen.

The beloved "Monkey Orchestra." Some may find it stuffy and old-fashioned, but I love it more than anything! That's why, for this table, I combined the "Monkey Orchestra" with "The Meissen Collage."

To keep it from looking stuffy I arranged everything on taupe table runners. For the flowers, I choose thistles. They look austere and give the lovely "Monkey Orchestra" figurines a more modern touch. The gold cutlery with the modern design goes well here. This is also a break, a mix of different styles that make a tablescape interesting.

Dragon meets Leopard

Weil ich diesen opulenten Mix so schön finde, habe ich ihn auch noch einmal draußen gedeckt. Der Clou: Auch die Stabkerzen haben noch unterschiedliche Farben. Die Kerzenhalter in Form eines „Äffchens" zaubern dem Betrachter ein Lächeln aufs Gesicht.

Because I find this opulent mix so beautiful, I chose to set another table with it, this time outdoors. The highlight: Even the candles are different colors. The candlesticks in the shape of a little monkey bring a smile to the face of the viewer.

Altes Porzellan, stylisch und modern gedeckt. Vom „Reichen Drachen“ in Gelb habe ich sechs Vorspeisenteller, so dass ich dieses Geschirr auch mal einfarbig decken kann.

Allerdings habe ich keine Hauptspeisenteller mit dem Dekor und so kombiniere ich sie wieder mit schlichten Tellern mit Goldrand von Limoges.

Da ich Gegensätze und Brüche auf dem Tisch wie in der Mode liebe, dekoriere ich „spacige“ Blumenvasen in Gold in Form eines Starmans dazu. Die Vasen habe ich in einer Galerie entdeckt. Ich finde sie so cool! Sie bieten zu dem alten Porzellan genau den richtigen Kontrast. Stylisch und außergewöhnlich. Dazu ist eine Blumendekoration nicht notwendig. Das schlichte Besteck in Gold und die Tischsets in Leinen in Gelb von Gabriele Hofer machen das Bild insgesamt modern.

Old porcelain used in a stylish, modern way. I have six appetizer plates from the “Rich Dragon” collection in yellow, which means I can sometimes use this tableware for a monochrome table.

However, I don’t have any dinner plates in this design, so here I once again combined them with sleek white plates with a gold rim from Limoges.

Since I love contrasts and breaks on the table (just like in fashion), I decorated the table with “spacey” gold astronaut vases. I discovered the vases in a gallery. I think they are so cool! They also provide just the right contrast to the old porcelain. Stylish and extraordinary. No flowers are needed for this table. The simple cutlery in gold and the yellow linen placemats from Gabriele Hofer make the picture altogether modern.

Golden Starman

Symphonie of blue and white

Wie bereits erwähnt mochte ich eine lange Zeit blau-weißes Geschirr gar nicht mehr. Aber heute ... ob das Zwiebelmuster von Meissen, Royal Copenhagen oder Bleus d'Aliieurs von Hermès: Ich liebe sie alle!

Diese Teller von Botessi habe ich in Lissabon auf einer Kunstreise entdeckt. Ganz schlicht habe ich sie ohne Tischwäsche auf unserem Marmortisch im Wohnzimmer gedeckt und mit dem Zwiebelmuster von Meissen und wieder einmal mit meinen schlichten Limoges Tellern gemixt.

Das goldene Besteck passt zu den Goldelementen in den Vorspeisentellern. Aber auch Silberbesteck würde gut passen. Immer öfter essen wir einfach mal am Wohnzimmertisch, wenn wir zu zweit sind.

As I already mentioned, for a long time I was not a fan of blue-and-white porcelain. But today, whether it's Meissen's classic "Blue Onion" pattern, Royal Copenhagen, or "Bleus d'Ailleurs" from Hermès, I love them all!

I discovered these plates by Botessi in Lisbon on an art tour. Very simple, I set them without table linens on our marble table in the living room and mixed them with the "Blue Onion" pattern from Meissen and once again with my plain Limoges plates.

The gold flatware matches the gold elements in the appetizer plates. But silverware would also go well. More and more often we just eat at the living room table when there are two of us.

To my Mother-in-law

Dieses Porzellan hat mein Mann von seiner Mutter geerbt.

Lange stand es im Keller in Kartons. Aber auch dieses Geschirr hat ein zweites Leben verdient! Ich habe es auf Tischläufern und Bastsets dekoriert. Die farblich verschiedener Kerzen in Silberleuchtern nehmen die Farbe des Geschirrs genauso wie die Hortensien auf. Die Windlichter in Rosa/Pink und der Porzellan-Kakadu geben dem alten Geschirr einen modernen Touch.

My husband inherited this porcelain from his mother.

For a long time, it languished in boxes in the basement. But this china also deserves a second life! I combined it with table runners and woven placemats. The different colored candles in silver candlesticks mirror the color of the pink candleholders and the porcelain cockatoo give the old dishes a modern touch.

Carlo Este

Discreet shades of green

Auf weißer Tischdecke mag ich die zeitgenössische Serie Carlo Este der Porzellanmanufaktur Fürstenberg am liebsten. Die taupefarbenen Tischläufer harmonieren wunderbar zu den hellen Türkis-/Grüntönen und den geometrischen Mustern des Porzellans und machen den Gesamteindruck modern. Schlichter, weißer Blumenschmuck, verteilt auf verschiedene kleine Vasen, und die Porzellanpapageien unterstreichen die edle Anmutung dieses Geschirrs.

On a white tablecloth, I like the contemporary "Carlo Este" series from Fürstenberg best. The taupe table runners harmonize wonderfully with the light turquoise/green tones and the geometric patterns of the porcelain, creating a modern overall impression. Simple white floral decorations, distributed among various small vases, and the porcelain parrots underline the elegant look of this tableware.

Die Serie Carlo Este passt wunderbar ins Frühjahr und den Sommer. Aber auch zu Weihnachten, mit weißen Christrosen dekoriert, mag ich dieses Dekor besonders gerne.

The "Carlo Este" series is perfect for spring and summer, but I also love using this porcelain at Christmas on a table decorated with white Christmas roses.

The taupe-colored table runners harmonize wonderfully with the light turquoise/green tones.

When everything flows

Hier wirkt das auf Farbflächen basierende Dekor für sich. Durch die Überlagerung der Bemalung entstehen neue Farben und Farbkombinationen. Das mit dem German Design Award ausgezeichnete Dekor Fluen Shifting Colors von Fürstenberg wirkt am schönsten, wenn es für sich steht. Im Fluss ohne Schnickschnack. Am liebsten mag ich das Service auf einer Marmorplatte oder auf einem modernen Holztisch.

This color blocks of this design speak for themselves. New colors and color combinations are created by overlapping the paint on the porcelain. The "Fluen Shifting Colors" collection from Fürstenberg, which won the German Design Award, looks best when it stands on its own. All flow, no frills. I like the service best on a marble slab or on a modern wooden table.

Sommerlich poppig. Auf einem weißen Tischläufer und Bastsets habe ich das blau-weiße Hermès Porzellan Bleus d'Aliieurs gedeckt. Hortensien in Pink und Blau sowie Servietten, Serviettenringe und Wassergläser in Pink machen den Tisch fröhlich und frisch.

Die Schalen und die Wasserkaraffe in Rotgold geben der Dekoration eine edle Anmutung.

Pink & blue. Summery poppy. I set the blue-and-white Hermès "Bleus d'Allieurs" porcelain on a white table runner with woven placemats. Hydrangeas in pink and blue, and napkins, napkin rings, and water glasses in pink make the table cheerful and fresh.

The bowls and water carafe in rose gold give the decoration a an elegant look.

Summery poppy

Sweet style is back.

Bestickte Tischdecken, Sets und Servietten sind wieder total en vogue!

Embroidered tablecloths, placemats, and napkins are totally en vogue again!

Epilogue

STORIES ABOUT TABLE COUTURE FOR HOSTS AND GUESTS

BY INGO KABUTZ

Werde auch du Table Couturier
You, too, can become a Table Couturier

Dein neues Kreativfeld für eigene Idee
A new creative field for your unique ideas

»Gute Mahlzeiten in guter Gesellschaft“ ist der dem Menschen mögliche Genuss einer gesitteten Glückseligkeit«

Immanuel Kant (1724 - 1804

“A good meal in good company is the enjoyment of a civilized bliss possible to man.”

Warum liegt es uns am Herzen, was treibt uns an, dir mit TABLE COUTURE einen Styleguide für die Neuinszenierung von Porzellan anzubieten? Was sind unsere Vorbilder, Werte und Orientierungspunkte? Wofür steht TABLE COUTURE und was möchte sie dir bieten?

Styleguide für deine eigene Tischkultur

Kurz gesagt möchten wir mit dir unsere Lust und Leidenschaft für innovative, stilvoll-edel gedeckte Tische teilen – und neu erlebbar machen. Wir möchten dich dazu „anstiften“, selbst kreativ zu werden. Mit einem Mix and Match aus altem und neuem Porzellan, Gläsern, Dekorationselementen, Blumen und Tischwäsche. Wir wünschen uns, dass alle, die sich angesprochen fühlen, selbst zu TABLE COUTURIERS werden. Und wir würden uns sehr freuen, würdest du über deine eigenen Kreationen berichten – und dich mit uns und weiteren „TABLE COTURIERS“ über neue individuelle „Table Kreationen“ austauschen.

Why is it so important to us, what is it that drives us to bring you TABLE COUTURE – a style guide for the restaging of porcelain? What are our sources of inspiration, our values, and our points of reference? What does TABLE COUTURE stand for and what does it offer you?

A style guide for the art of entertaining

In short, we would like to share with you our desire and passion for innovative, elegantly stylish table settings – and let you experience them in a new way. We would like to inspire you to become creative yourself. With a mix and match of old and new porcelain, glasses, decorative elements, flowers, and table linens. We hope that everyone who feels that this book speaks to them will also become “Table Couturiers” themselves. And we would be very pleased if you would report on your own creations and share your ideas for new, personalized tablescapes with us and other Table Couturiers.

Wir möchten vor allem aber auch die junge Generation für die neu definierte Tischkultur begeistern. Wir empfinden es als unsere Aufgabe, mit TABLE COUTURE dazu beizutragen, dass junge Leute die Tischkultur frühzeitig als ein „nachhaltiges Kreativfeld für eigene Ideen" entdecken und in ihre Alltags- und Festtagskultur fest einbinden.

Above all, we would like to inspire the younger generation to become enthusiastic about this redefined art of entertaining. With TABLE COUTURE, our goal is to help young people discover the art of entertaining early on as a "sustainable creative field for their own unique ideas" and to firmly integrate it into their lives – both day to day and on special occasions.

Das Kreativfeld, das in dein Leben passt

Ein Kreativfeld, das mit seinen Möglichkeiten und Werten in das Leben der neuen Generation passt. Einer Generation, für die Luxus nur wenig mit Preis, Prestige und Besitz der Gegenstände zu tun hat, sondern vor allem mit ihren kulturellen und nachhaltigen Werten. Und natürlich hat es für diese neuen Luxus-Konsumenten eine Bedeutung, dass sie mit der TABLE COUTURE auch einen Beitrag zur Umwelt- und Ressourcenschonung leisten.

A creative field that fits into your life

The art of entertaining is a creative field that, with all of its possibilities and values, is the perfect match for a new generation. A generation for whom luxury has little to do with price, prestige, or possessing objects, but rather above all with their cultural and sustainable values. And, of course, these new luxury consumers also feel it is important to contribute to environmental protection and resource conservation with TABLE COUTURE.

»Die Esslust ist die direkte und robuste Empfindung eines Bedürfnisses, dem man genügt. Tafelfreude hingegen ist eine ‚reflektierte Empfindung', keimend aus den verschiedensten Umständen des Ortes, der Atmosphäre, der Personen und der schönen Dinge, die beim Mahle mitwirken«

Jean Anthèlme Brillat-Savarin (1755 -1826)

"The pleasure of eating is the actual and direct sensation of satisfying a need, while the pleasures of the table are a reflective sensation which is born from the various circumstances of place, time, things, and people who make up the surroundings of the meal."

So nachhaltig ist die TABLE COUTURE
Sustainability and TABLE COUTURE

Mix and Match – Pluspunkte für die Umwelt
Mix and match – advantageous for the environment

Mix and Match Table Settings mit altem und neuem Porzellan aus Manufakturen – und mit einem „guten grünen Gewissen"? Nachhaltigkeit ist für uns alle ein wichtiger Wert. Deshalb ist es vorab gut zu wissen, dass es zu Porzellan als Gebrauchsgegenstand in puncto Umwelt- und Ressourcenschonung keine wirklichen Alternativen gibt.

Zwar wird bei näherer Betrachtung des Herstellungsprozesses deutlich, dass die Produktion von Porzellan sehr hohe Brenntemperaturen – und somit sehr viel Energie braucht. Womit Porzellan dann allerdings innerhalb der Ökobilanz die entscheidenden Pluspunkte macht, ist die Langlebigkeit. Und damit erscheinen Aufwendungen für Energieressourcen in einem ganz anderen Licht.

Porzellan hat eine fast unbegrenzte Lebensdauer

Porzellan ist bekannt für eine unbegrenzte Lebensdauer. Das gilt insbesondere für die handbemalte Luxusklasse. Denn diese Gedecke, Figuren und

Mixed and matched table settings that combine old and new porcelain from different manufacturers – and it's good for the environment? Sustainability is an important topic for all of us. That's why it's good to know in advance that there are no real alternatives to porcelain as a commodity in terms of environmental protection and resource conservation.

A closer look at the manufacturing process reveals that the production of porcelain requires very high firing temperatures – and thus a lot of energy. However, what gives porcelain the decisive advantage in terms of life cycle is its durability. This puts the amount of energy required to manufacture porcelain in a completely different light.

Porcelain has an almost unlimited lifespan

Porcelain is known for its unlimited lifespan. This is especially true for the hand-painted luxury class. That's because these dishes, figurines, and other precious pieces

»Vor dem Gesetz und bei Tische haben alle die gleichen Rechte und gleiche Pflichten. Die Tafel macht uns alle gleich« ***Grimod de la Reynière (1758-1837***

"Before the law and at the table, we all have the same rights and the same obligations. The table is the great equalizer."

anderen wertvollen Stücke werden von ihren stolzen Besitzern akribisch gehütet und gepflegt, und von Generation zu Generation weitergegeben. Tatsächlich teilen heute Porzellansammler weltweit ihre Leidenschaft für die Ikonen „aus weißem Gold" der Edel-Manufakturen.

Neues Leben für alte Stücke

Edelporzellane, wie wir sie in unserem TABLE COUTURE Styleguide inszenieren, werden sorgfältig aufgehoben. Und da wir aktuelle und neue Kreationen mit älteren Porzellanen oder Einzelstücken aus dem Bestand matchen, reaktivieren wir auch die „alten", teils nicht mehr vollständigen Stücke. So retten wir Porzellane, aber auch Gläser, Dekorationselemente, Tischtücher und andere Accessoires und verleihen ihnen ein neues Leben. Unser Motto: Mit Leidenschaft immer wieder gern eine neue Edel-Porzellanserie erwerben. Aber – die alten vorhandenen Stücke weiterhin wertschätzen und neu inszenieren.

So nachhaltig ist die TABLE COUTURE.

are meticulously protected and cared for by their proud owners, and passed down from generation to generation. Indeed, today porcelain collectors around the world share their passion for these icons made of "white gold" from the finest manufacturers.

New life for old pieces

Precious porcelain, like the pieces we stage in our TABLE COUTURE style guide, is carefully preserved. And, since we match current and new creations with older porcelain or individual pieces from our collections, we also reactivate these "old" pieces, some of which are no longer complete. In this way, we rescue not only porcelain dishes, but also glasses, decorative elements, tablecloths, and other accessories and give them a new life. Our motto: We are passionate about porcelain and are always happy to acquire an exquisite new dishware set. But, at the same time, we also continue to value and restage our older pieces as well.

Who knew TABLE COUTURE could be so sustainable?

Für den Titel unseres Coffee Table Books „TABLE COUTURE" steht die Haute Couture – die hohe Schneiderkunst – natürlich als Vorbild. Jeder weiß: Die Haute Couture ist die Königsdisziplin der Mode. Der Begriff selbst bezieht sich auf luxuriöse, maßgeschneiderte Kleidung, die unter Verwendung hochwertigster Materialien und künstlerischer Techniken hergestellt wird. Die maßgefertigten, hochexklusiven Roben entstehen in feinster Handarbeit.

Und ja … Porzellan und die hohe Schneiderkunst weisen beide Merkmale einer gemeinsamen Identität auf.

Viele Gemeinsamkeiten bei den Kreativ- und Fertigungsschritten

Anlässlich der Ausstellung „Porcelain Couture – Porzellan trifft Mode von Chanel bis Yves Saint Laurent im Museum Schloss Fürstenberg" im Herbst 2018 stellt der Designer und Ko-Kurator Peter Kempe fest: „Luxus-Porzellan und Haute Couture werden in vergleichbaren Arbeitsschritten gefertigt. Somit haben sie auch Gemeinsamkeiten. Damit meine ich, dass der ganze Fertigungsprozess auf beiden Seiten sehr zeitaufwendig ist. Das ist ganz viel Handarbeit. Bei einem Chanel-Kostüm wird beispielsweise extra der Stoff gewebt, oder Knöpfe entworfen – das ist bei Porzellan genauso."

Haute Couture und Luxus-Porzellan haben also eine gemeinsame Identität: die Liebe zum Detail, das meisterhafte Handwerk, das Streben nach Perfektion und die Exklusivität.

For the title of our coffee table book TABLE COUTURE, haute couture – the high art of tailoring – naturally served as our inspiration. Everyone knows: Haute couture is the supreme discipline of fashion. The term itself refers to luxurious, bespoke clothing made using the highest quality materials and artistic techniques. The highly exclusive custom-made gowns are painstakingly crafted by hand.

And yes ... china and the high art of tailoring both exhibit characteristics of a common identity.

Many commonalities in terms of creativity and manufacture

On the occasion of the exhibition "Porcelain Couture – Porcelain Meets Fashion from Chanel to Yves Saint Laurent" at Museum Schloss Fürstenberg in fall 2018, designer and co-curator Peter Kempe stated: "The steps involved in making luxury porcelain and haute couture are comparable. Thus, they also have commonalities. By that I mean that the entire manufacturing process is very time-consuming on both sides. It's a lot of manual work. With a Chanel suit, for example, the fabric is specially woven, or buttons are designed – it's the same with porcelain."

And so haute couture and luxury porcelain have a common identity: attention to detail, masterful craftsmanship, the pursuit of perfection, and exclusivity.

Haute Couture und Porzellan

Haute couture and porcelain

Die gemeinsame Identität der Haute Couture und Porzellan

The common identity of haute couture and luxury porcelain

Schöne Dinge des kunstvoll gedeckten Tisches „mitessen“

“Consuming” the beautiful objects on an artfully decorated table

Vom Wert des Speisens in einer ästhetischen Umgebung

On the value of dining in an aesthetically pleasing environment

Im Dialog mit den Gedanken des japanischen Philosophen Tadashi Ogawa

In dialogue with the thoughts of the Japanese philosopher Tadashi Ogawa

Der japanische Philosoph Tadashi Ogawa hilft uns zu verstehen, was ein sorgfältig und liebevoll gedeckter Tisch in uns auslöst. Vor allem dann, wenn der Tisch und die Umgebung auch noch eine als wohltuend und „gastlich“ empfundene Atmosphäre ausstrahlen.

Denn in Japan wie in Europa und auch in fast allen anderen Teilen der Welt ist das „geheiligte Erlebnis“ des gemeinsamen Essens in der Familie nahezu verschwunden. Im Sinne des japanischen Begriffs „Ko-sho-ku“, nehmen viele Kinder zu Hause ein „einsames Essen“ ein. Ebenso die Eltern. Zunehmend findet die tägliche Hauptmahlzeit nicht mehr in familiärer Atmosphäre statt, sondern als Fast-Food in jedweder Form. Wie aber können wir das fortschreitende Fehlen dieses identitätsbildenden Rituals ausgleichen?

The Japanese philosopher Tadashi Ogawa helps us to understand what a carefully and lovingly laid table elicits in us. Especially when the table and the surroundings also radiate an atmosphere that is perceived as pleasant and “hospitable.”

In Japan, as in Europe and in almost every other part of the world, the “sacred experience” of eating together as a family has almost disappeared. Today many children – and many parents – have a “solitary meal” at home. The Japanese term for this is “koshoku.” More and more, the main daily meal no longer takes place in a family atmosphere, but rather as fast food in any form. But how can we compensate for the growing absence of this identity-forming ritual?

Fast Food – Slow Food

Folgen wir den Gedanken Ogawas: Er versteht das Zusammenspiel von „Essen und Atmosphäre“ als ein Wesen der Esskultur. In seinem Buch „Grund und Grenze des Bewußtseins“ beschreibt Ogawa das Essen als eine kulturelle Lebenspraxis der Menschen und lenkt die Aufmerksamkeit auf die Unterschiede zwischen einem schnellen Essen (Fast Food) und einem langsamen Essen (Slow Food).

Im Dialog mit Tadashi Ogawa

Worin liegt der persönliche Stellenwert des Essens an einer gemeinsamen Tafel, und insofern der Wert einer TABLE COUTURE? Warum genießen wir es so sehr, an einem schön gedeckten Tisch Platz zu nehmen? Letztlich geht es Ogawa um die Wiedergewinnung des Essens als „Genuß ... in einem ästhethischen Rahmen“.

Schöne Dinge des kunstvoll gedeckten Tisches „mitessen“

Diejenige Form der Nahrungsaufnahme verdient laut Ogawa besondere Aufmerksamkeit, die bereits Aristoteles kannte: Slow Food.

Ogawa beschreibt unter Berufung auf Aristoteles, dass durch die Kultivierung einer langsamen Mahlzeit die Aufmerksamkeit nicht nur auf das Essen als Nahrungsaufnahme beschränkt ist, sondern die ganze Atmosphäre der Situation wahrgenommen und um ihrer selbst willen genossen wird: An einem sorgfältig gedeckten Tisch, etwa in einem Restaurant oder bei einer privaten Einladung.

Fast food, slow food

Let us follow Ogawa's thoughts: He understands the interplay of "food and atmosphere" as the essence of food culture. In his book Foundation and Limits of Consciousness – Intercultural Phenomenology from a Japanese Perspective, Ogawa describes food as a cultural practice in our everyday lives and draws attention to the differences between a fast meal (fast food) and a slow meal (slow food).

In dialogue with Tadashi Ogawa

What is the personal value of eating at a communal table, and thus the value of a TABLE COUTURE? Why do we enjoy sitting down at a beautifully set table as much as we do? Ultimately, Ogawa is concerned with the recovery of eating as "enjoyment ... in an aesthetically pleasing setting."

"Consuming" beautiful objects on the artfully decorated table

According to Ogawa, slow food is a form of eating that dates all the way back to Aristotle – and one that deserves special attention.

Citing Aristotle, Ogawa claims that by cultivating slow eating, our attention is not limited to the food itself strictly for the purpose of food intake, but rather we perceive and enjoy the whole atmosphere of the situation for its own sake: at a carefully decorated table, for example in a restaurant or at someone's home.

Itadaki
masu
"I thank you for
the food" Ancient
Japanese
grace
„Ich bedanke mich für
die Mahlzeit“ Altes
japanisches
Tischgebet

ANG!

Style & Icons

Bernardaud
Bitossi
Cavalli
Dior
Engels Kerzen
Franzen
Fornasetti
Fürstenberg
Gabriele Hofer
Ginori
Hermès
Jars Céramistes
Jeff Koons
John Derian & Astier de Villatte
Jonathan Adler
Kartell
LaDoubleJ
Lalique
Lucie Kaas
Meissen
Reichenbach
Riedel
Royal Copenhagen
Rotter Glas
Sieger by Fürstenberg
Victor Breuer
Zalto

Bernardaud

www.bernardaud.com

Bitossi Home

www.butossihome.it

Victor Breuer

www.victorbreuer.de

Roberto Cavalli

www.robertocavalli.com

Dior Maison

www.dior.com

Engels Kerzen

www.engels-kerzen.de

Franzen

www.franzen.de

Fornasetti

www.fornasetti.com

Fürstenberg
wwwfuerstenberg-porzellan.com

Ginori 1735
www.ginori1735.com

Hermès

www.hermes.com

Gabriele Hofer

www.gabriele-hofer.de

Jars Céramistes

www.jarsceramistes.com

Jeff Koons

www.jeffkoons.com

John Derian

www.johnderian.com

Jonathan Adler

www.jonathanadler.com

Kartell

www.kartell.com

LaDoubleJ

www.ladoublej.com

Lalique

www.lalique.com

Limoges

www.bernardaud.com

Lucie Kaas

www.luciekaas.com

Meissen

www.meissen.com

Reichenbach

www.porzellanmanufaktur.net

Riedel

www.riedel.com

Royal Copenhagen

www.royalcopenhagen.com

Rotter Glas

www.rotter-glas.de

Sieger by Fürstenberg

www.sieger-germany.com

Zalto

www.zaltoglas.at

TheCreatives

Petra Dieners
Fashion Blogger, Designer,
Entrepreneur
Düsseldorf / Germany

info@lieblingsstil.com
www.lieblingsstil.com
instagram.com/petradieners
instagram.com/
puretoi_petradieners

Ingo Kabutz
Brand + Research Consultant,
Creative Director, Publisher
Düsseldorf / Germany

i.kabutz@stella-publishing.de
www.stella-publishingl.de
Follow me at LinkedIn

Ansgar Bolle
Photographer, Designer,
Communication Consultant
Düsseldorf / Germany

info@ansgarbolle.de
www.ansgarbolle.de
www.instagram.com/
ansgarbollephotography/

Uwe Erensmann
Photographer

Düsseldorf / Germany

presse@erensmann.de
instagram.com/uweerensmann/

Erwin Wenzel
Photographer

Düsseldorf / Germany

fotos@erwinwenzel.de
www.erwinwenzel.de
instagram.com/
erwinwenzel.photographer/

Imprint

1st edition September 2023

Author: Petra Dieners
Epilogue: Ingo Kabutz

TABLE COUTURE is an international registered and protected Trademark of Petra Dieners & Ingo Kabutz.

Concept:
Petra Dieners & Ingo Kabutz
Creative Direction:
Ingo Kabutz
Lithography:
Timo Wojciechowski

Copy writing Table Couture:
Petra Dieners
Copy writing Epilogue: Ingo Kabutz
Copy editing, Translation: Anne Fries, Düsseldorf

Printing Company:
Appl Druck, Wemding, Germany

Photo Credits:

Erwin Wenzel:
Cover, Pages 4, 6, 7, 10, 12/13, 14/15, 18/19, 20/21, 227, 231, 242,

Uwe Erensmann:
Page 124 - 127, 237

Ansgar Bolle:
All other pages

»Sage mir, wie du isst,
und ich sage dir, was du bist«

Jean Anthèlme Brillat-Savarin
(1755 -1826)

"Tell me what you eat,
and I will tell you who you are."